1000 FACTS ON
SCIENCE AND
TECHNOLOGY

First published by Miles Kelly Publishing Ltd
Bardfield Centre, Great Bardfield
Essex, CM7 4SL

Editor
Belinda Gallagher

Assistant Editor
Mark Darling

Art Director
Clare Sleven

Designer
Phil Kay

Picture Research
Liberty Newton

British Library Cataloguing-in-Publication Data
A catalogue record for this book is available from the British Library

ISBN 1-84236-053-1

Printed in Hong Kong

www.mileskelly.net
info@mileskelly.net

1000 FACTS ON
SCIENCE AND TECHNOLOGY

$E = MC^2$

John Farndon
Consultant Steve Parker

Miles Kelly
PUBLISHING

Contents

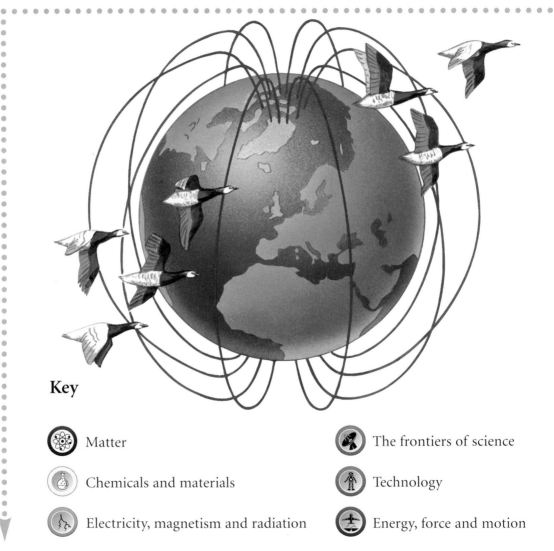

Key

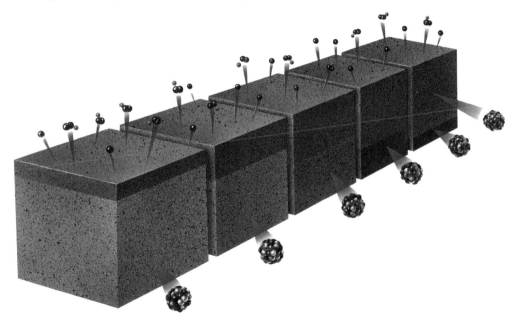

Contents

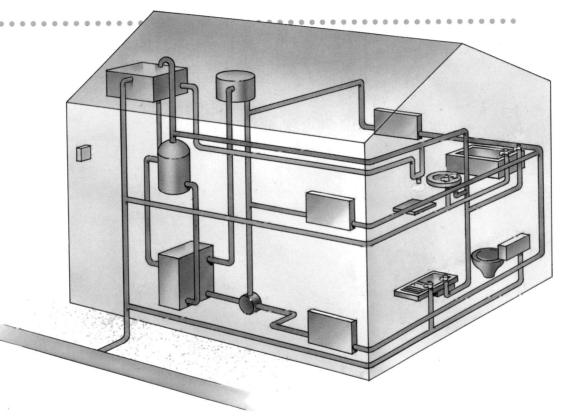

Elements

- **Elements** are the basic chemicals of the Universe. Each element is made from only one kind of atom, with a certain number of sub atomic particles and its own unique character.

- **More than 115** elements have so far been identified.

- **Each element** is listed in the periodic table.

- **At least 20** of the most recently identified elements were created entirely by scientists and do not exist naturally.

- **All the most recently discovered elements** have very large, heavy atoms.

- **The lightest atom** is hydrogen.

- **The densest naturally occurring atom** is osmium.

- **When different elements combine** they make chemical compounds (see chemical compounds).

- **New elements** get their name from their atomic number (see the Periodic Table). So the new element with atomic number 116 is called ununhexium. *Un* is the Latin word for one; *hex* is Latin for six.

▲ *Very few elements occur naturally by themselves. Most occur in combination with others in compounds. Gold is one of the few elements found as a pure 'native' element.*

▶ *Silver is a chemical element. It is a soft, white metal which is used for jewellery and also in dentistry, medicine, photography and electronics.*

▲ As the demand for aluminium grows each year with more and more uses being found for it, so recycling becomes ever more important.

▲ Aluminium is used to make drink cans since it is a light weight metal that does not rust and resists wear from weather or chemicals.

...**FASCINATING FACT**...
Scientists in Berkeley, California, have made three atoms of a new element 118 or, ununoctium, which is probably a colourless gas.

9

Atoms

- **Atoms are** tiny particles which build together to make every substance. An atom is the tiniest bit of any pure substance or chemical element.

- **You could fit** two billion atoms on the full stop after this sentence.

- **The number of atoms** in the Universe is about 10 followed by 80 zeros.

- **Atoms are mostly** empty space dotted with a few even tinier particles called subatomic particles.

- **In the centre** of each atom is a dense core, or nucleus, made from two kinds of particle: protons and neutrons. Protons have a positive electrical charge, and neutrons none. Both protons and neutrons are made from different combinations of quarks (see quarks).

- **If an atom** were the size of a sports arena, its nucleus would be just the size of a pea.

- **Around the nucleus** whizz even tinier, negatively-charged particles called electrons (see electrons).

- **Atoms can be split** but they are usually held together by three forces: the electrical attraction between positive protons and negative electrons, and the strong and weak 'nuclear' forces that hold the nucleus together.

- **Every element** is made from atoms with a certain number of protons in the nucleus. An iron atom has 26 protons, gold has 79. The number of protons is the atomic number.

- **Atoms with the same number** of protons but a different number of neutrons are called isotopes.

▶ *The nucleus of an atom is made up of two kinds of particle: protons (red) and neutrons (green). Protons have a positive electric charge while neutrons have none. Tiny electrons (blue) whizz around the nucleus.*

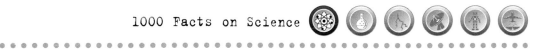

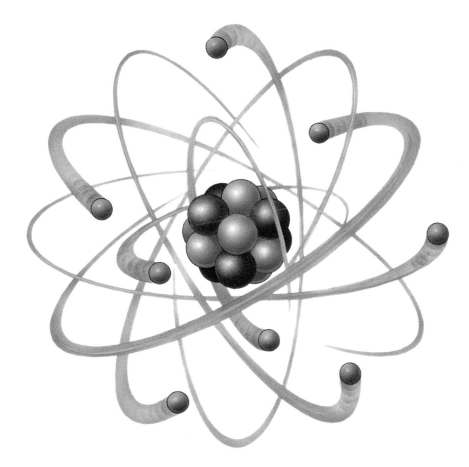

Electrons

- **Electrons** are by far the smallest of the three main, stable parts of every atom; the other two parts are protons and neutrons (see atoms). In a normal atom there are the same number of electrons as protons.

- **Electrons** are 1836 times as small as protons and have a mass of just 9.109×10^{-31} kg. 10^{-31} means there are 30 zeros after the decimal point. So they weigh almost nothing.

- **Electrons were discovered** by English physicist Joseph John Thomson in 1897 as he studied the glow in a cathode-ray tube (see television). This was the first time anyone realized that the atom is not just one solid ball.

▼ *Each atom has a different number of electrons. Its chemical character depends on the number of electrons in its outer shell. Atoms with only one electron in their outer shell, such as lithium, sodium and potassium, have many properties in common. The electron shell structures for five common atoms are shown here.*

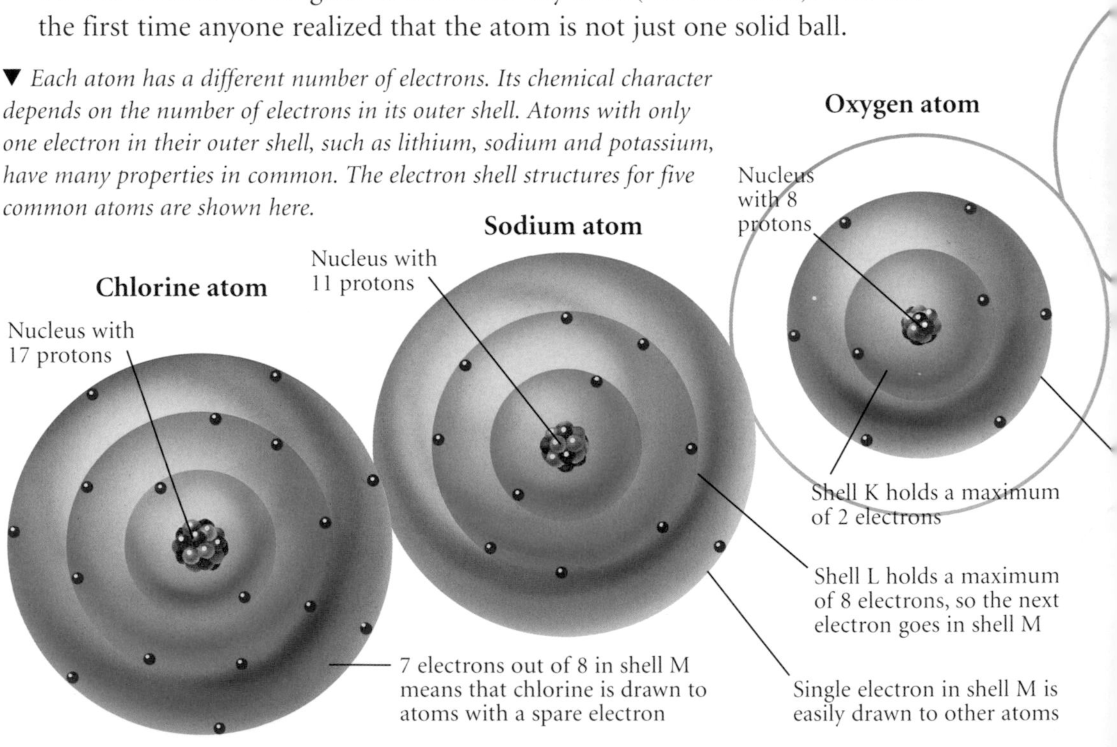

Oxygen atom

Nucleus with 8 protons

Sodium atom

Nucleus with 11 protons

Chlorine atom

Nucleus with 17 protons

Shell K holds a maximum of 2 electrons

Shell L holds a maximum of 8 electrons, so the next electron goes in shell M

7 electrons out of 8 in shell M means that chlorine is drawn to atoms with a spare electron

Single electron in shell M is easily drawn to other atoms

12

Hydrogen atom

Single electron

Nucleus with single proton

Carbon atom

Nucleus with 6 protons

Maximum 2 electrons in shell K

Shell L holds 4 electrons out of a possible 8. So carbon has four vacancies to form complex compounds with other elements

Shell L holds 6 electrons out of a possible 8. So oxygen has 2 'missing' electrons and is very reactive

● **Electrons are** packets of energy. They can be thought of either as a tiny vibration or wave, or as a ball-like particle. They travel as waves and arrive as particles.

● **You can never be sure** just where an electron is. It is better to think of an electron circling the nucleus not as a planet circling the Sun but as a cloud wrapped around it. Electron clouds near the nucleus are round, but those farther out are other shapes, such as dumb-bells.

● **Electrons** have a negative electrical charge. This means they are attracted to positive electrical charges and pushed away by negative charges. 'Electron' comes from the Greek word for amber. Amber tingles electrically when rubbed.

● **Electrons cling** to the nucleus because protons have a positive charge equal to the electron's negative charge.

● **Electrons have so much energy** that they whizz round too fast to fall into the nucleus. Instead they circle the nucleus in shells (layers) at different distances, or energy levels, depending on how much energy they have. The more energetic an electron, the farther from the nucleus it is. There is room for only one other electron at each energy level, and it must be spinning in the opposite way. This is called Pauli's exclusion principle.

● **Electrons are** stacked around the nucleus in shells, like the layers of an onion. Each shell is labelled with a letter and can hold up to a particular number of electrons. Shell K can hold up to 2, L 8, M 18, N 32, O about 50, and P about 72.

13

Molecules

- **A molecule** is two or more atoms bonded together. It is normally the smallest bit of a substance that exists independently.

- **Hydrogen atoms** exist only in pairs, or joined with atoms of other elements. A linked pair of hydrogen atoms is a hydrogen molecule.

- **The atoms in a molecule** are held together by chemical bonds (see chemical bonds).

- **The shape of a molecule** depends on the arrangement of bonds that hold its atoms together.

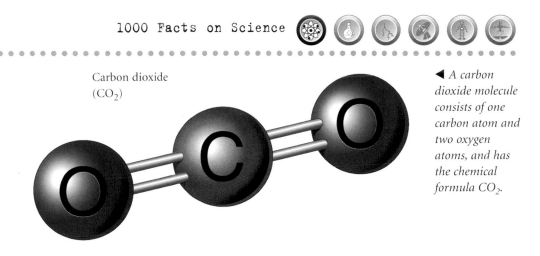

Carbon dioxide
(CO_2)

◀ *A carbon dioxide molecule consists of one carbon atom and two oxygen atoms, and has the chemical formula CO_2.*

- **Ammonia molecules** are pyramid shaped; some protein molecules are long spirals.

- **Compounds** only exist as molecules. If the atoms in the molecule of a compound were separated, the compound would cease to exist.

- **Chemical formulas** show the atoms in a molecule.

- **The formula for ammonia,** a kind of gas, is NH_3 – one nitrogen atom and three hydrogen.

- **The mass of a molecule** is called the molecular mass. It is worked out by adding the mass of all the atoms in it.

◀ *A crystal such as this is built from billions of identical molecules.*

. . . **FASCINATING FACT** . . .
If the DNA molecule in every human body cell were as thick as a hair, it would be eight km long.

Chemical bonds

- **Chemical bonds** link together atoms to make molecules (see molecules).

- **Atoms can bond** in three main ways: ionic bonds, covalent bonds and metallic bonds.

- **In ionic bonds** electrons are transferred between atoms.

- **Ionic bonds** occur when atoms with just a few electrons in their outer shell give the electrons to atoms with just a few missing from their outer shell.

- **An atom** that loses an electron becomes positively charged; an atom that gains an electron becomes negatively charged so the two atoms are drawn together by the electrical attraction of opposites.

- **Sodium** loses an electron and chlorine gains one to form the ionic bond of sodium chloride (table salt) molecules.

- **In covalent bonding,** the atoms in a molecule share electrons.

- **Because they are negatively** charged, the shared electrons are drawn equally to the positive nucleus of both atoms involved. The atoms are held together by the attraction between each nucleus and the shared electrons.

- **In metallic bonds** huge numbers of atoms lose their electrons. They are held together in a lattice by the attraction between 'free' electrons and positive nuclei.

> ...FASCINATING FACT...
> Seven elements, including hydrogen, are
> found in nature only as two atoms
> covalently bonded.

▶ *In this carbon dioxide molecule the carbon is held to two oxygen atoms by covalent bonds.*

◀ *Each of the four hydrogen atoms in methane (CH_4) shares its electron with the central carbon atom to create strong covalent bonds.*

17

The Periodic Table

- **The Periodic Table** is a chart of all the 100-plus different chemical elements.

- **The Periodic Table** was devised by Russian Dmitri Mendeleyev. He realized that each element is part of a complete set, and so he predicted the existence of three then unknown elements – gallium, scandium and germanium.

- **The Periodic Table** arranges the elements according to their Atomic Number, which is the number of protons in their atoms (see atoms). The table lists the elements in order of Atomic Number, starting with hydrogen at 1.

- **Atoms** usually have the same number of electrons as protons. So the Atomic Number also indicates the normal number of electrons an atom has.

- **Atomic mass** is the average weight of an atom of an element and corresponds to the average number of protons and neutrons in the nucleus. The number of neutrons varies in some atoms so the atomic mass is never a round number.

- **Columns** in the Periodic Table are called Groups. Rows are called Periods.

- **The number** of electron layers (shells) in the atoms of an element increases by one down each Group. The elements in each Period have the same number of electron shells.

- **The electrons** in the atom's outer shell increases by one across each Period.

- **Each Group** is made up of elements with a certain number of electrons in their outer shell. This is what largely determines the element's character. All the elements in each Group have similar properties. Many of the Groups have a name as well as a number, as shown opposite.

- **Each Period** starts on the left with a highly reactive alkali metal of Group 1, such as sodium. Each atom of elements in Group 1 has an electron in its outer shell. Each Period ends on the right with a 'noble' gas of Group 0, such as argon. These elements have the full number of electrons in their outer shell and do not react.

Groups

1

Above the name for each element is its abbreviation, or 'formula'.

Below the name for each element is the Atomic Number.

These elements (green) are called poor metals.

These elements (sand-coloured) are called non-metals.

As Atomic Numbers increase by one along each period, so chemical properties change.

2

0

3 4 5 6 7

H Hydrogen 1																		He Helium 2
Li Lithium 3	Be Beryllium 4											B Boron 5	C Carbon 6	N Nitrogen 7	O Oxygen 8	F Fluorine 9	Ne Neon 10
Na Sodium 11	Mg Magnesium 12											Al Aluminium 13	Si Silicon 14	P Phosphorus 15	S Sulphur 16	Cl Chlorine 17	Ar Argon 18
K Potassium 19	Ca Calcium 20	Sc Scandium 21	Ti Titanium 22	V Vanadium 23	Cr Chromium 24	Mn Manganese 25	Fe Iron 26	Co Cobalt 27	Ni Nickel 28	Cu Copper 29	Zn Zinc 30	Ga Gallium 31	Ge Germanium 32	As Arsenic 33	Se Selenium 34	Br Bromine 35	Kr Krypton 36
Rb Rubidium 37	Sr Strontium 38	Y Yttrium 39	Zr Zirconium 40	Nb Niobium 41	Mo Molybdenum 42	Tc Technetium 43	Ru Ruthenium 44	Rh Rhodium 45	Pd Palladium 46	Ag Silver 47	Cd Cadmium 48	In Indium 49	Sn Tin 50	Sb Antimony 51	Te Tellurium 52	I Iodine 53	Xe Xenon 54
Cs Caesium 55	Ba Barium 56		Hf Hafnium 72	Ta Tantalum 73	W Tungsten 74	Re Rhenium 75	Os Osmium 76	Ir Iridium 77	Pt Platinum 78	Au Gold 79	Hg Mercury 80	Tl Thallium 81	Pb Lead 82	Bi Bismuth 83	Po Polonium 84	At Astatine 85	Rn Radon 86
Fr Francium 87	Ra Radium 88		Rf Rutherfordium 104	Db Dubnium 105	Sg Seaborgium 106	Bh Bohrium 107	Hs Hassium 108	Mt Meitnerium 109	Uun Ununnilium 110	Uuu Unununium 111	Uub Ununbium 112						

La Lanthanum 57	Ce Cerium 58	Pr Praseodymium 59	Nd Neodymium 60	Pm Promethium 61	Sm Samarium 62	Eu Europium 63	Gd Gadolinium 64	Tb Terbium 65	Dy Dysprosium 66	Ho Holmium 67	Er Erbium 68	Tm Thulium 69	Yb Ytterbium 70	Lu Lutetium 71
Ac Actinium 89	Th Thorium 90	Pa Protactinium 91	U Uranium 92	Np Neptunium 93	Pu Plutonium 94	Am Americium 95	Cm Curium 96	Bk Berkelium 97	Cf Californium 98	Es Einsteinium 99	Fm Fermium 100	Md Mendelevium 101	No Nobelium 102	Lr Lawrencium 103

The final Group (Group 0) on the right is the noble gases.

Group 1 is called alkali metals. They are all soft, very reactive metals.

Group 2 is the alkaline–earth group. They occur naturally only in compounds.

The block in the middle (purple) is transition metals such as gold and copper.

This row, called the lanthanides, or rare earths, fits into Group 3. All are shiny metals.

This row, called the actinides, fits into Group 3. It includes radium and plutonium.

▲ *There are eight columns, or Groups, across in the Periodic Table and seven rows, or Periods, down. The block of transition metals in the middle fits into Group 3. Each element has three electrons in its outer shell, but different numbers in the inner shells.*

Lavoisier

- **Antoine Laurent Lavoisier** (1743–1794) was a brilliant French scientist who is regarded as the founder of modern chemistry.

- **He was elected** to the French Royal Academy of Sciences at just 25 for an essay on street lighting. A year later, he worked on the first geological map of France.

- **Lavoisier earned his living** for a long while as a 'tax farmer', which meant he worked for a private company collecting taxes.

- **In 1771** he married 14-year-old Marie Paulze, who later became his illustrator and collaborator in the laboratory.

▲ *Lavoisier showed the importance of precision weighing in the laboratory.*

- **Lavoisier** was the first person to realize that air is essentially a mixture of two gases: oxygen and nitrogen.

- **Lavoisier discovered** that water is a compound of hydrogen and oxygen.

- **Lavoisier** showed that the popular phlogiston theory of burning was wrong and that burning involves oxygen instead.

▶ *Lavoisier showed that old theories about burning were wrong and that oxygen is essential in order for burning to take place.*

● **Lavoisier** gave the first working list of chemical elements in his famous book *Elementary Treatise of Chemistry* (1789), which was illustrated by his wife Marie.

● **From 1776** Lavoisier headed research at the Royal Arsenal in Paris, developing gunpowder manufacture.

● **Lavoisier ran schemes** for public education, fair taxation, old-age insurance and other welfare schemes. But his good deeds did not save him. When Lavoisier had a wall built round Paris to reduce smuggling, revolutionary leader Marat accused him of imprisoning Paris's air. His past as a tax farmer was remembered and Lavoisier was guillotined in 1794.

Hydrogen

- **Hydrogen** is the lightest of all gases and of all elements. An Olympic-size swimming pool full of hydrogen would weigh just 1 kg.

- **Hydrogen** is the smallest and simplest of all atoms, with just one proton and one electron.

- **Hydrogen** is the first element in the Periodic Table. It has an Atomic Number of 1 and an atomic mass of 1.00794.

- **One in every 6000** hydrogen atoms has a neutron as well as a proton in its nucleus, making it twice as heavy. This heavy hydrogen atom is called deuterium.

- **Very rare** hydrogen atoms have two neutrons as well as the proton, making them three times as heavy. These are called tritium.

- **Hydrogen** is the most common substance in the Universe, making up over 90% of the Universe's weight.

◄ *Hydrogen's combination with oxygen in water makes it one of the most important elements on the Earth.*

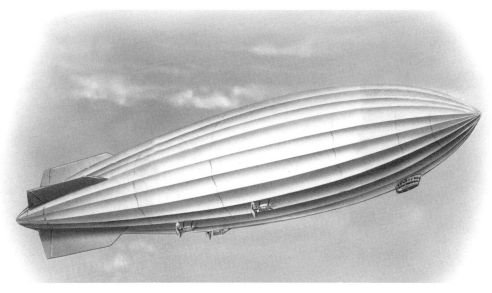

▲ *In 1937, the hydrogen used to lift the airship* Hindenburg *ignited, killing many of the ship's passengers. Eventually, non-flammable helium was used in airships.*

- **Hydrogen** was the first element to form, soon after the Universe began. It was billions of years before any other element formed.

- **Most hydrogen** on Earth occurs in combination with other elements, such as oxygen in water. Pure hydrogen occurs naturally in only a few places, such as small underground pockets and as tiny traces in the air.

- **Hydrogen** is one of the most reactive gases. It bursts easily and often explosively into flames.

- **Under extreme pressure** hydrogen becomes a metal – the most electrically conductive metal of all.

23

Nitrogen

- **Nitrogen** is a colourless, tasteless, odourless, inert (unreactive) gas, yet it is vital to life.

- **Nitrogen is** 78.08% of the air.

- **Nitrogen** turns liquid at −196°C and freezes at −210°C.

- **Liquid nitrogen** is so cold that it can freeze organic substances so quickly they suffer little damage.

- **Food such as cheesecakes** and raspberries are preserved by being sprayed with liquid nitrogen.

▲ *On average 100 kg of nitrate fertilizer are used on every hectare of farmland in the world to replace nitrogen taken from the soil by crops.*

- **Nitrogen combines** with oxygen to form compounds such as nitrates.

- **Nitrogen and oxygen** compounds are an essential ingredient of the proteins and nucleic acids from which all living cells are made.

- **Lightning makes** 250,000 tonnes of nitric acid a day. It joins nitrogen and oxygen in the air to make nitrogen oxide.

- **On a long sea dive,** the pressure in a diver's lungs makes extra nitrogen dissolve in the blood. If the diver surfaces too quickly the nitrogen forms bubbles, giving 'the bends', which can be painful or even fatal.

▲ *Nitrogen-frozen raspberries. Although expensive, this method freezes food faster and better than air-blast and indirect-contact methods.*

...**FASCINATING FACT**...
When they die, some people have their bodies frozen with liquid nitrogen in the hope that medical science will one day bring them back to life.

Oxygen

- **Oxygen** is the second most plentiful element on Earth, making up 46% of the Earth's crust. Air is 20.94% oxygen.

- **Oxygen** is one of the most reactive elements. This is why oxygen in the Earth's crust is usually found joined with other chemicals in compounds.

- **Oxygen has an atomic number** of 8 and an atomic weight of 15.9994.

- **Oxygen molecules** in the air are made from two oxygen atoms; three oxygen atoms make the gas ozone.

- **Oxygen turns to a pale blue liquid** at −182.962°C. It freezes at −218.4°C.

Acetylene cylinder   Oxygen cylinder

▲ *Oxyacetylene torches produce an extremely hot flame for welding and cutting materials. By combining oxygen and acetylene the torch can produce a flame of around 3300°C.*

- **Most life depends on oxygen** because it joins with other chemicals in living cells to give the energy needed for life processes. The process of using oxygen in living cells is called cellular respiration.

- **Liquid oxygen,** or LOX, is combined with fuels such as kerosene to provide rocket fuel.

- **Oxygen** was discovered independently by Carl Scheele and Joseph Priestley during the 1770s.

- **The name** 'oxygen' means acid-forming. It was given to the gas in 1779 by Antoine Lavoisier (see Lavoisier).

▲ *Oxygen is needed for combustion to take place. Substances such as wood give off heat with a flame when they burn, while others, such as charcoal, give off heat with a faint glow.*

. . . **FASCINATING FACT** . . .
The oxygen in the air on which your life depends was produced mainly by algae.

27

Air

- **The air** is a mixture of gases, dust and moisture.

- **The gas nitrogen** makes up 78.08% of the air. Nitrogen is largely unreactive, but it sometimes reacts with oxygen to form oxides of nitrogen.

- **Nitrogen** is continually recycled by the bacteria that consume plant and animal waste.

- **Oxygen** makes up 20.94% of the air. Animals breathe in oxygen. Plants give it out as they take their energy from sunlight in photosynthesis.

- **Carbon dioxide** makes up 0.03% of the air. Carbon dioxide is continually recycled as it is breathed out by animals and taken in by plants in photosynthesis.

- **The air contains** other, inert (unreactive) gases: 0.93% is argon; 0.0018% is neon; 0.0005% is helium.

- **There are tiny traces** of krypton and xenon which are also inert.

- **Ozone makes up** 0.00006% of the air. It is created when sunlight breaks up oxygen.

- **Hydrogen makes up** 0.00005% of the air. This gas is continually drifting off into space.

▶ *People often think that air is largely made up of oxygen. In fact, only 21% of air is oxygen while 78% of it is nitrogen.*

......FASCINATING FACT....
Air is a unique mixture that exists on Earth and nowhere else in the Solar System.

▶ *Air is the mixture of gases that surrounds the Earth and is contained in the atmosphere. Clouds form when large masses of moist air rise and cool.*

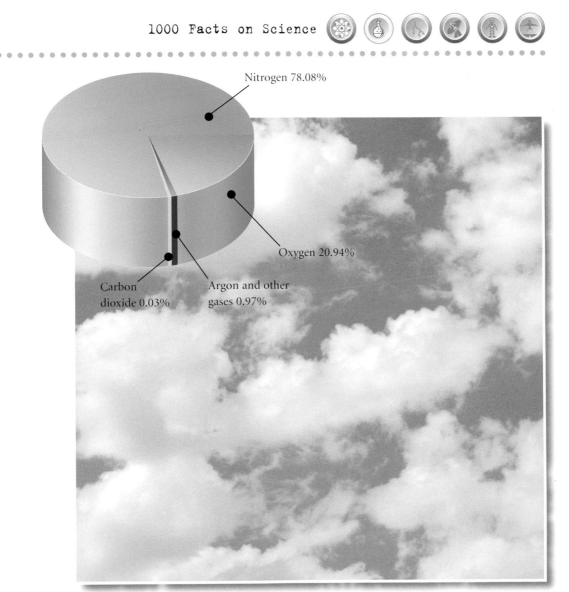

Nitrogen 78.08%

Oxygen 20.94%

Carbon
dioxide 0.03%

Argon and other
gases 0.97%

Carbon

▶ *The extraordinary hardness of diamonds comes from the incredibly strong tetrahedron (pyramid shape) that carbon atoms form.*

- **Pure carbon** occurs in four forms: diamond, graphite, amorphous carbon and fullerenes.

- **Fullerenes** are made mostly artificially, but all four forms of carbon can be made artificially.

- **Diamond** is the world's hardest natural substance.

- **Natural diamonds** were created deep in the Earth billions of years ago. They were formed by huge pressures as the Earth's crust moved, and then brought nearer the surface by volcanic activity.

- **Graphite** is the soft black carbon used in pencils. It is soft because it is made from sheets of atoms that slide over each other.

- **Amorphous carbon** is the black soot left behind when candles and other objects burn.

▲ *The pencil is the most widely used writing instrument in the world. Astronauts use pencils in space because they are not affected by gravity or pressure.*

30

- **Fullerenes** are big molecules made of 60 or more carbon atoms linked together in a tight cylinder or ball. The first was made in 1985.

- **Fullerenes** are named after the architect Buckminster Fuller who designed a geodesic (Earth-shaped) dome.

- **Carbon forms** over one million compounds which are the basis of organic chemistry. It does not react chemically at room temperature. Carbon has the chemical formula C and the atomic number 6. Neither diamond nor graphite melts at normal pressures.

▲ *Diamonds are crystals made up almost entirely of carbon. They occur in various shapes and sizes, and were formed under great heat and pressure.*

···**FASCINATING FACT**···
All living things are based on carbon, yet it makes up just 0.032% of the Earth's crust.

Water

- **Water is the only substance** that is solid, liquid and gas within the natural range of Earth temperatures. It melts at 0°C and boils at 100°C.

- **Water is at its densest** at 4°C.

- **Ice is much less dense** than water, which is why ice forms on the surface of ponds and why icebergs float.

- **Water is one of the few substances** that expands as it freezes, which is why pipes burst during cold winter weather.

- **Water has a unique capacity** for making mild solutions with other substances.

- **Water is a compound** made of two hydrogen atoms and one oxygen atom. It has the chemical formula H_2O.

- **A water molecule** is shaped like a flattened V, with the two hydrogen atoms on each tip.

▲ A water molecule has two hydrogen atoms and one oxygen atom in a shallow V-shape.

▲ Water is found in liquid form in many places, such as rivers, and as a gas in the atmosphere.

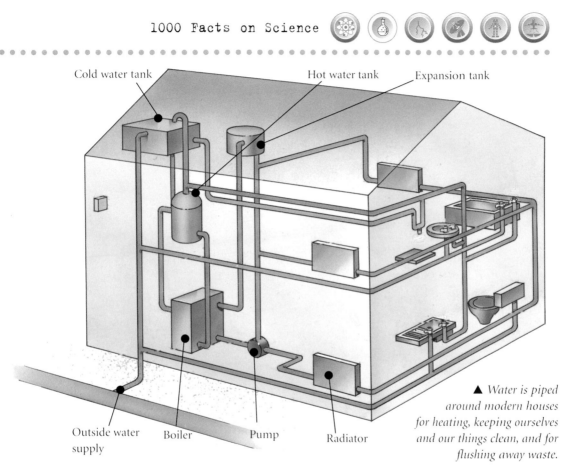

Cold water tank

Hot water tank

Expansion tank

Outside water supply

Boiler

Pump

Radiator

▲ *Water is piped around modern houses for heating, keeping ourselves and our things clean, and for flushing away waste.*

- **A water molecule** is said to be polar because the oxygen end is more negatively charged electrically.

- **Similar substances** such as ammonia (NH_3) are gases to below 0°C.

- **Water stays liquid** until 100°C because pairs of its polar molecules make strong bonds, as the positively charged end of one molecule is drawn to the negatively charged end of another.

Oil

- **Oils** are liquids that do not dissolve in water and burn easily.

- **Oils are usually made** from long chains of carbon and hydrogen atoms.

- **There are three main kinds of oil:** essential, fixed and mineral oils.

- **Essential oils** are thin, perfumed oils from plants. They are used in flavouring and aromatherapy.

- **Fixed oils** are made by plants and animals from fatty acids. They include fish oils and nut and seed oils.

- **Mineral oils** come from petroleum formed underground over millions of years from the remains of micro-organisms.

- **Petroleum,** or crude oil, is made mainly of hydrocarbons. These are compounds made only of hydrogen and carbon, such as methane (see oil compounds).

- **Hydrocarbons** in petroleum are mixed with oxygen, sulphur, nitrogen and other elements.

- **Petroleum** is separated by distillation into various substances such as aviation fuel, petrol or gasoline and paraffin. As oil is heated in a distillation column, a mixture of gases evaporates. Each gas cools and condenses at different heights to a liquid, or fraction, which is then drawn off.

▶ *Oil from underground and undersea sediments provides over half the world's energy needs.*

FASCINATING FACT
Petroleum is used to make products from aspirins and toothpaste to CDs, as well as gasoline, or petrol.

▲ *From oil comes petrol and other fuels, which can be burned to release their fossil energy. The oil has to go through a processing stage before it can be used.*

Oil compounds

- **Hydrocarbons** are compounds made only of carbon and hydrogen atoms. Most oil products are hydrocarbons.

- **The simplest hydrocarbon** is methane, the main gas in natural gas (and flatulence from cows!). Methane molecules are one carbon atom and four hydrogen atoms.

- **Alkanes or paraffins** are a family of hydrocarbons in which the number of hydrogen atoms is two more than twice the number of carbon atoms.

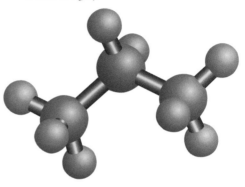

▼ *This is a propane molecule. The carbon atoms are purple, the hydrogen atoms are grey.*

- **Lighter alkanes** are gases such as methane and propane which make good fuels.

- **Candles** contain a mixture of alkanes.

- **Alkenes or olefins** are a family of hydrocarbons in which there are twice as many hydrogen atoms as carbon atoms.

◀ *PVC is a vinyl plastic used for making rainmacs. It is a hydrocarbon with chlorine atoms added.*

- **The simplest alkene** is ethene, also called ethylene (C_2H_4) which is used to make polythene and other plastics such as PVC.

- **Green bananas and tomatoes** are often ripened rapidly in ripening rooms filled with ethene.

- **Ethene** is the basis of many paint strippers.

- **Ethene** can be used to make ethanol, the alcohol in alcoholic drinks.

▲ *In an oil refinery, crude oil is broken down into an enormous range of different hydrocarbons.*

Metals

▲ *Mercury, sometimes known as quicksilver, expands by a relatively large amount when warmed, and so is widely used to measure temperature.*

- **75% of all known elements** are metals.

- **Most metals** ring when hit. A typical metal is hard but malleable, which means it can be hammered into thin sheets.

- **Metals** are usually shiny. They conduct both heat and electricity very well.

- **Metals** do not form separate molecules. Instead atoms of metal knit together with metallic bonds (see chemical bonds) to form lattice structures.

- **The electron shells of all metals** are less than half-full. In a chemical reaction metals give up their electrons to a non-metal.

▲ *Metals are very tough but can be easily shaped. They are used for an enormous variety of things, from chains to cars.*

▶ *Molten gold is poured into moulds at a smelting plant. When the bullion cools, it forms bars that are about 99.99% pure. These are stored in strong vaults.*

- **Most metals** occur naturally in the ground only in rocks called ores.

- **Gold, copper,** mercury, platinum, silver and a few other rare metals occur naturally in their pure form.

- **Mercury** is the only metal that is liquid at normal temperatures. It melts at −38.87°C.

- **A few atoms** of the new metal ununquadium (atomic number 114) were made in January 1999.

... FASCINATING FACT ...
At 3410°C, tungsten has the highest
melting point of any metal.

Calcium

- **Calcium** is a soft, silvery white metal. It doesn't occur naturally in pure form.

- **In compounds,** calcium is the fifth most abundant element on the Earth.

- **Calcium** is one of six alkaline-earth metals.

- **Most calcium compounds** are white solids called limes. They include chalk, porcelain, tooth enamel, cement, seashells, the limescale on taps.

- **The word 'lime'** comes from the Latin word for 'slime'.

- **Quicklime** is calcium oxide. It is called 'quick' (Old English for 'living') because when water drips on it, it twists and swells as if it is alive.

▲ *Calcium is one of the basic building materials of living things. It is one of the crucial ingredients in shell, such as those on crabs, and bone, which is why they are typically white.*

- **Slaked lime** is calcium hydroxide. It may be called 'slaked' because it slakes (quenches) a plant's thirst for lime in acid soils.

- **Calcium has** an atomic number of 20. It has a melting point of 839°C and a boiling point of 1484°C.

- **Limelight** was the bright light used by theatres in the days before electricity. It was made by applying a mix of oxygen and hydrogen to pellets of calcium.

- **Calcium adds rigidity** to bones and teeth and helps to control muscles. Your body gets it from milk and cheese.

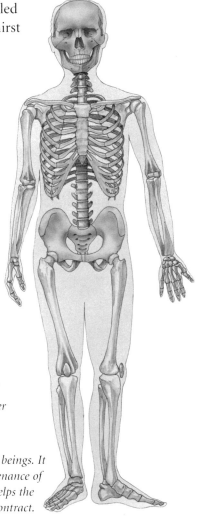

◀▲ *Milk and its products, such as butter and cheese, are key sources of calcium. Green vegetables are another important source.*

▶ *Calcium is essential to human beings. It is vital for the growth and maintenance of the bones and teeth, and it also helps the blood to clot and the muscles to contract.*

Iron and steel

- **Iron** is the most common element in the world. It makes up 35% of the Earth, but most of it is in the Earth's core.

- **Iron is never found** in its pure form in the Earth's crust. Instead it is found in iron ores, which must be heated in a blast furnace to extract the iron.

- **The chemical symbol** for iron is Fe from *ferrum*, the Latin word for iron. Iron compounds are called either ferrous or ferric.

- **Iron has** an atomic number of 26 and an atomic weight of 55.85.

- **Iron melts** at 1535°C and boils at 3000°C. It conducts heat and electricity quite well and dissolves in water very slowly. Iron is easily magnetized. It also loses its magnetism easily, but steel can be permanently magnetic.

- **Iron** combines readily with oxygen to form iron oxide, especially in the presence of moisture. This is rusting.

◀ *Pouring molten iron into a steelmaking furnace in a steel mill. The temperature of the liquid metal is about 1500°C.*

▶ *A solid-state laser can cut through carbon steel like butter even though steel is incredibly tough.*

- **Cast iron** is iron with 2 to 4% carbon and 1 to 3% silicon. It is suitable for pouring into sand moulds. Wrought iron is almost pure iron with carbon removed to make it easy to bend and shape for railings and gates.

- **Iron is made into steel** by adding traces of carbon for making cars, railway lines, knives and much more. Alloy steels are made by adding traces of metals such as tungsten (for tools) and chromium (for ball bearings).

- **60% of steel** is made by the basic oxygen process in which oxygen is blasted over molten iron to burn out impurities.

- **Special alloy steels** such as chromium steels can be made from scrap iron (which is low in impurities) in an electric arc furnace.

43

Aluminium

- **Aluminium** is by far the most common metal on the Earth's surface. It makes up 8% of the Earth's crust.

- **Aluminium** never occurs naturally in its pure form; in the ground it is combined with other chemicals as minerals in ore rocks.

- **The major source** of aluminium is layers of soft ore called bauxite, which is mostly aluminium hydroxide.

▶ *Half of the soft drinks cans in the USA are made from recycled aluminium.*

- **Alum powders** made from aluminium compounds were used 5000 years ago for dyeing. Pure aluminium was first made in 1825 by Danish scientist Hans Oersted.

- **Aluminium** production was the first industrial process to use hydroelectricity when Paul Héroult set up a plant on the river Rhine in 1887.

- **Aluminium is silver** in colour when freshly made, but it quickly tarnishes to white in the air. It is very slow to corrode.

- **Aluminium** is one of the lightest of all metals. It weighs just one-third as much as steel.

- **Aluminium oxide** can crystallize into one of the hardest minerals, corundum, which is used to sharpen knives.

- **Aluminium** melts at 650°C and boils at 2450°C.

- **Each year 21 million tonnes** of aluminium are made, mostly from bauxite dug up in Brazil and New Guinea.

◀ *Although aluminium is common in the ground, it is worth recycling because extracting it from bauxite uses a lot of energy.*

Copper

▲ *The high conductivity of copper makes it a perfect material for the core of electrical cables.*

- **Copper** was one of the first metals used by humans over 10,000 years ago.

- **Copper** is one of the few metals that occur naturally in a pure form.

- **Most of the copper** that we use today comes from ores such as cuprite and chalcopyrite.

- **The world's biggest deposits** of pure copper are in volcanic lavas in the Andes Mountains in Chile.

- **Copper has** the atomic number 29, an atomic mass of 63.546 and melts at 1083°C.

- **Copper is** by far the best low-cost conductor of electricity, so it is widely used for electrical cables.

- **Copper is also** a good conductor of heat, which is why it is used to make the bases of saucepans and heating pipes.

- **Copper is so ductile** (easily stretched) that a copper rod as thick as a finger can be stretched out thinner than a human hair.

- **After being in the air** for some time, copper gets a thin green coating of copper carbonate called verdigris. '*Verdigris*' means green of Greece.

▲ *Copper utensils on sale.*
Copper not only withstands heat
but is an attractive material to
have in people's homes.

> **FASCINATING FACT**
> Copper is mixed with tin to make
> bronze, the oldest of all alloys dating
> back more than 5000 years.

47

Crystals

- **Crystals** are particular kinds of solids that are made from a regular arrangement, or lattice, of atoms. Most rocks and metals are crystals, so are snowflakes and salt.

- **Most crystals** have regular, geometrical shapes with smooth faces and sharp corners.

- **Most crystals** grow in dense masses, as in metals. Some crystals grow separately, like grains of sugar.

- **Some crystals** are shiny and clear to look at. Crystals got their name from the chunks of quartz that the ancient Greeks called krystallos. They believed the chunks were unmeltable ice.

- **Crystals** form by a process called crystallization. As liquid evaporates or molten solids cool, the chemicals dissolved in them solidify.

- **Crystals** grow gradually as more and more atoms attach themselves to the lattice, just as icicles grow as water freezes onto them.

- **The smallest crystals** are microscopically small. Occasionally crystals of a mineral such as beryl may grow to the size of telegraph poles.

- **A liquid crystal** is a crystal that can flow like a liquid but has a regular pattern of atoms.

- **A liquid crystal** may change colour or go dark when the alignment of its atoms is disrupted by electricity or heat. Liquid crystal displays (LCDs) use a tiny electric current to make crystals affect light.

- **X-ray crystallography** uses x-rays to study the structure of atoms in a crystal. This is how we know the structure of many important life substances such as DNA.

▲ *Crystals such as these grow naturally as minerals and are deposited from hot mineral-rich liquids underground.*

Organic chemistry

◀ *All living things are made basically of carbon compounds.*

- **Organic chemistry** is the study of compounds that contain carbon atoms.

- **Over 90%** of all chemical compounds are organic.

- **Organic chemicals** are the basis of most life processes.

- **Scientists once thought** carbon compounds could only be made by living things. However, in 1828 Friedrich Wöhler made the compound urea in his laboratory.

- **By far the largest** group of carbon compounds are the hydrocarbons (see oil).

- **Aliphatic organic compounds** are formed from long or branching chains of carbon atoms. They include ethane, propane and paraffin, and the alkenes from which many polymers are made (see oil compounds).

- **Cyclic organic compounds** are formed from closed rings of carbon atoms.

- **Aromatics** are made from a ring of six atoms (mostly carbon), with hydrogen atoms attached. They get their name from the strong aroma (smell) of benzene.

- **Benzene** is the most important aromatic. Friedrich Kekuleé von Stradowitz discovered benzene's six-carbon ring structure in 1865, after dreaming about a snake biting its own tail.

- **Isomers** are compounds with the same atoms but different properties. Butane and 2-methyl propane in bottled gas are isomers.

▲ *A giant container containing butane, a colourless, flammable gas used for fuel.*

51

Acids and alkalis

- **Mild acids,** such as acetic acid in vinegar, taste sour.

- **Strong acids,** such as sulphuric acid, are highly corrosive. They dissolve metals.

- **Acids** are solutions that are made when certain substances containing hydrogen dissolve in water.

- **Hydrogen atoms** have a single electron. When acid-making substances dissolve in water, the hydrogen atoms lose their electron and become positively charged ions. Ions are atoms that have gained or lost electrons.

▲ *Citrus fruits such as oranges, lemons and limes have a tart taste because they contain a mild acid, called citric acid. It has a pH of 3.*

- **The strength of an acid** depends on how many hydrogen ions form.

- **The opposite of an acid** is a base. Weak bases such as baking powder taste bitter and feel soapy. Strong bases such as caustic soda are corrosive.

- **A base that dissolves** in water is called an alkali. Alkalis contain negatively charged ions – typically ions of hydrogen and oxygen, called hydroxide ions.

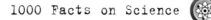
- **When you add an acid** to an alkali, both are neutralized. The acid and alkali react together forming water and a salt.

- **Chemists** use indicators such as litmus paper to test for acidity. Acids turn litmus paper red. Alkalis turn it blue. The strength of an acid may be measured on the pH scale. The strong acid (laboratory hydrochloric) has a pH of 1. The strongest alkali has a pH of 14. Pure water has a pH of about 7 and is neutral – neither acid nor alkali.

▲ *Water, with its neutral pH of 7, is safe for people to wash themselves with or to drink.*

◀ *Some batteries are made from alkaline cells. These contain a strong alkali solution such as potassium hydroxide which conducts electricity very effectively, making such batteries a strong source of energy.*

> . . . **FASCINATING FACT** . . .
> Hydrochloric acid in the stomach (with a pH of 1 to 2) is essential for digestion.

Soaps

- **Some soaps** are natural; all detergents are synthetic.

- **All soaps and detergents** clean with a 'surfactant'.

- **Surfactants** are molecules that attach themselves to particles of dirt on dirty surfaces and lift them away.

- **Surfactants** work because one part of them is hydrophilic (attracted to water) and the other is hydrophobic (repelled by water).

- **The hydrophobic tail** of a surfactant digs its way into the dirt; the other tail is drawn into the water.

▼ *Surfactant molecules in soap lift dirt off dirty surfaces.*

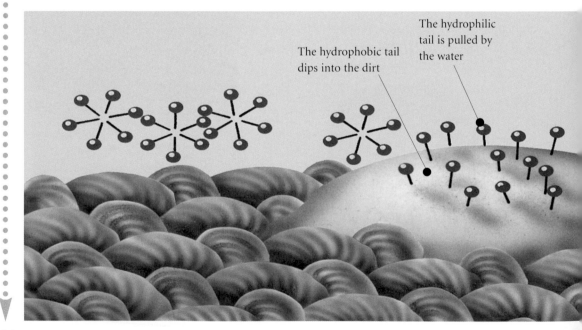

The hydrophilic tail is pulled by the water

The hydrophobic tail dips into the dirt

- **Soaps** increase water's ability to make things wet by reducing the surface tension of the water.

- **Soap** is made from animal fats or vegetable oil combined with chemicals called alkalis, such as sodium or potassium hydroxide.

- **Most soaps** include perfumes, colours and germicides (germ-killers) as well as a surfactant.

- **The Romans used** soap over 2000 years ago.

- **Detergents** were invented in 1916 by German chemist, Fritz Gunther.

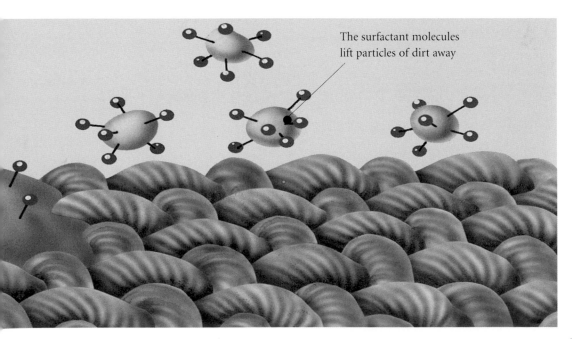

The surfactant molecules lift particles of dirt away

55

Halogens

- **Halogens** are the chemical elements fluorine, chlorine, bromine, iodine and astatine.

- **The word 'halogen'** means salt-forming. All halogens easily form salt compounds.

- **Many of the salts in the sea** are compounds of a halogen and a metal, such as sodium chloride and magnesium chloride.

- **The halogens** all have a strong, often nasty, smell.

- **Fluorine** is a pale yellow gas, chlorine a greenish gas, bromine a red liquid, and iodine a black solid.

- **Astatine** is an unstable element that survives by itself only briefly. It is usually made artificially.

◀ *Chlorine salts are often added to the water in swimming pools to kill bacteria, giving the water a greenish-blue tinge.*

▼ *Halogen lights floodlight a stadium at night, allowing large audiences to watch. Halogens are non-metals and make up part of the seventh main Group in the Periodic Table.*

- **The halogens** together form Group 7 of the Periodic Table, elements with 7 electrons in the outer shells.

- **Because halogens have** one electron missing, they form negative ions and are highly reactive.

- **The iodine and bromine** in a halogen lightbulb make it burn brighter and longer than a normal electric lightbulb.

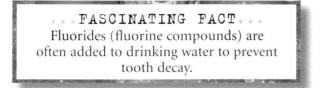
. . . FASCINATING FACT . . .
Fluorides (fluorine compounds) are often added to drinking water to prevent tooth decay.

Chemical compounds

- **Compounds** are substances that are made when the atoms of two or more different elements join together.

- **The properties of a compound** are usually very different from those of the elements which it is made of.

- **Compounds** are different from mixtures because the elements are joined together chemically. They can only be separated by a chemical reaction.

- **Every molecule** of a compound is exactly the same combination of atoms.

- **The scientific name** of a compound is usually a combination of the elements involved, although it might have a different common name.

- **Table salt** is the chemical compound sodium chloride. Each molecule has one sodium and one chlorine atom.

- **The chemical formula** of a compound summarizes which atoms a molecule is made of. The chemical formula for water is H_2O because each water molecule has two hydrogen (H) atoms and one oxygen (O) atom.

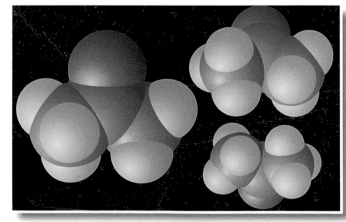

◀ *The molecules of a compound are identical combinations of atoms.*

▲ *Table salt, or sodium chloride, forms when sodium hydroxide neutralizes hydrocloric acid.*

- **There only 100 or so elements** but they can combine in different ways to form many millions of compounds.

- **The same combination of elements,** such as carbon and hydrogen, can form many different compounds.

- **Compounds** are either organic (see organic chemistry), which means they contain carbon atoms, or inorganic.

59

Chemical reactions

- **A candle burning,** a nail rusting, a cake cooking – all involve chemical reactions.

- **A chemical reaction** is when two or more elements or compounds meet and interact to form new compounds or separate out some of the elements.

- **The chemicals** involved in a chemical reaction are called the reactants. The results are called the products.

- **The products** contain exactly the same atoms as the reactants but in different combinations.

- **The products** have exactly the same total mass as the reactants. This is called conservation of mass.

- **Some reactions** are reversible, which means the products can be changed back to the original reactants. Others, such as making toast, are irreversible.

- **Effervescence** is a reaction in which gas bubbles form in a liquid, turning it fizzy.

- **A catalyst** is a substance that speeds up, slows down, or enables a chemical reaction to happen but remains unchanged at the end.

- **Nearly all reactions** involve energy. Some involve light or electricity. Most involve heat. Reactions that give out heat are called exothermic. Those that draw in heat are called endothermic.

- **Oxidation** is a reaction in which oxygen combines with a substance. Burning is oxidation; as the fuel burns it combines with oxygen in the air. Reduction is a reaction in which a substance loses its oxygen.

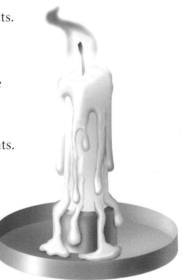

▼ *Candle wax contains a mixture of carbon and hydrogen. When lit, the melted wax is drawn up the wick and burns, using oxygen in the air.*

▲ *Burning is an oxidation reaction. Carbon in the trees combines with oxygen in the air to form carbon dioxide.*

Solutions

◀ *A cup of tea is made up of the solvent, water, and a number of solutes: the tea, milk and perhaps sugar. A highly saturated solution produces strong, sweet tea. A poorly saturated solution produces weak tea.*

● **Tap water** is rarely pure water; it usually contains invisible traces of other substances. This makes it a solution.

● **A solution** is a liquid that has a solid dissolved within it.

● **When a solid dissolves,** its molecules separate and mix completely with the molecules of the liquid.

● **The liquid** in a solution is called the solvent.

● **The solid** dissolved in a solution is the solute.

● **The more of a solid that dissolves,** the stronger the solution becomes until at last it is saturated and no more will dissolve. There is literally no more room in the liquid.

● **If a saturated** solution is heated the liquid expands, making room for more solute to dissolve.

- **If a saturated** solution cools or is left to evaporate there is less room for solute, so the solute is precipitated (comes out of the solution).

- **Precipitated solute** molecules often link together to form solid crystals.

▲ *Sea water is a solution containing a huge range of dissolved substances. They include simple salt (sodium chloride) and magnesium chloride, but most are in very tiny amounts.*

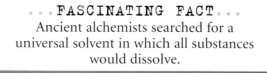

. . . **FASCINATING FACT** . . .
Ancient alchemists searched for a universal solvent in which all substances would dissolve.

Glass

- **Glass** is made mainly from ordinary sand (made of silica), from soda ash (sodium carbonate) and from limestone (calcium carbonate).

- **Glass** can be made from silica alone. However, silica has a very high melting point (1700°C), so soda ash is added to lower its melting point.

- **Adding a lot of soda ash** makes glass too soluble in water, so limestone is added to reduce its solubility.

- **To make sheets of glass,** 6% lime and 4% magnesia (magnesium oxide) are added to the basic mix.

▲ *Glass is one of the most versatile of all materials – transparent, easily moulded and resistant to the weather. This is why it is used in modern buildings such as this extension to the Louvre in Paris.*

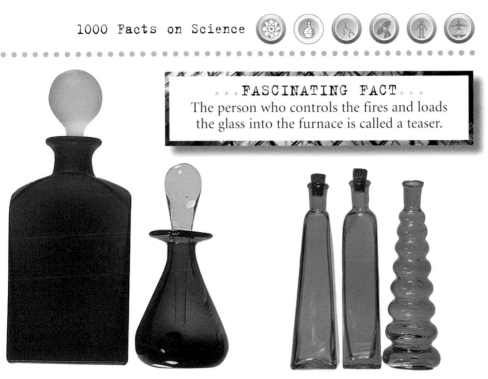

▲ *Certain oxides are added to glass to colour it. One part of nickel oxide in 50,000 produces a tint ranging from yellow to purple. One part of cobalt oxide in 10,000 gives an intense blue. Red glasses are made with gold, copper or selenium oxides.*

- **To make glass for bottles,** 2% alumina (aluminium oxide) is added to the basic mix.

- **Very cheap glass** is green because it contains small impurities of iron.

- **Metallic oxides** are added to make different colours.

- **Unlike most solids,** glass is not made of crystals and does not have the same rigid structure. It is called an amorphous solid.

- **When glass is very warm** it flows slowly like a very thick liquid.

Solids, liquids and gases

- **Most substances** can exist in three states – solid, liquid or gas. These are the states of matter.

- **Substances** change from one state to another at particular temperatures and pressures.

- **As temperature rises,** solids melt to become liquids. As it rises further, liquids evaporate to become gases.

- **The temperature** at which a solid melts is its melting point.

- **The maximum temperature** a liquid can reach before turning to gas is called its boiling point.

- **Every solid has strength** and a definite shape as its molecules are firmly bonded in a rigid structure.

- **A liquid has a fixed volume** and flows to take up the shape of any solid container into which it is poured.

▲ The grains of sand in this egg timer act like a liquid, taking on the shape of the glass as they flow from top to bottom.

- **A liquid flows** because although bonds hold molecules together, they are loose enough to move over each other, rather like dry sand.

- **A gas** such as air does not have any shape, strength or fixed volume. This is because its molecules are moving too quickly for any bonds to hold them together.

- **When a gas cools,** its molecules slow down until bonds form between them to create drops of liquid. This process is called condensation.

▲ *A giant iceberg floats on the sea. Although ice is lighter than water and looks so different, chemically it is exactly the same.*

New materials

- **Synthetic materials** are materials created by humans, such as plastics.

- **Many synthetic materials** are polymers. These are substances with chains of organic molecules made up from identical smaller molecules, monomers.

- **Some polymers** are natural, such as the plant fibre cellulose.

- **The first synthetic polymer** was Parkesine, invented by Alexander Parkes in 1862. The first successful synthetic polymer was celluloid, invented by John Hyatt in 1869 and soon used for photographic film.

- **Nylon** was the first fully synthetic fibre. It is a polymer created by Wallace Carothers of Du Pont in the 1930s.

◀ This phone was made from Bakelite, one of the earliest types of plastic.

- **PVC** is polyvinyl chloride, a synthetic polymer developed in the 1920s.

- **Composites** are new, strong, light materials created by combining a polymer with another material.

- **Carbon-reinforced plastic** consists of tough carbon fibres set within a polymer.

- **Kevlar** is a composite developed by Du Pont in 1971. It is made from nylon-like fibres set within a polymer.

▲ *Snowboards are made from composites such as Kevlar, which combine lightness with strength.*

...**FASCINATING FACT**...
New 'smart' materials might change their properties in response to conditions.

69

Plastics

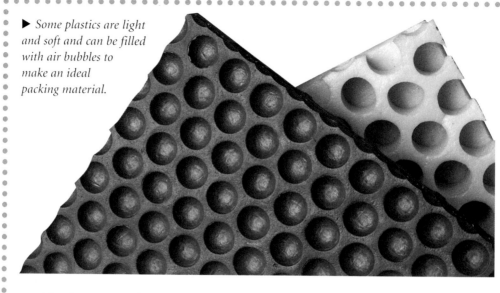

▶ *Some plastics are light and soft and can be filled with air bubbles to make an ideal packing material.*

- **Plastics are synthetic** (man-made) materials that can be easily shaped and moulded.

- **Most plastics are polymers** (see new materials). The structure of polymer molecules gives different plastics different properties.

- **Long chains of molecules** that slide over each other easily make highly flexible plastics such as polythene. Tangled chains make rigid plastics such as melamine.

- **Typically** plastics are made by joining carbon and hydrogen atoms. These form ethene molecules, which can be joined to make a plastic called polythene.

- **Many plastics** are made from liquids and gases that are extracted from crude oil.

- **Thermoplastics** are soft and easily moulded when warm but set solid when cool. They are used to make bottles and drainpipes and can be melted again.

- **Thermoset plastics,** which cannot be remelted once set, are used to make telephones and pan handles.

- **Blow moulding** involves using compressed air to push a tube of plastic into a mould.

- **Vacuum moulding** involves using a vacuum to suck a sheet of plastic into a mould.

- **Extrusion moulding** involves heating plastic pellets and forcing them out through a nozzle to give the required shape.

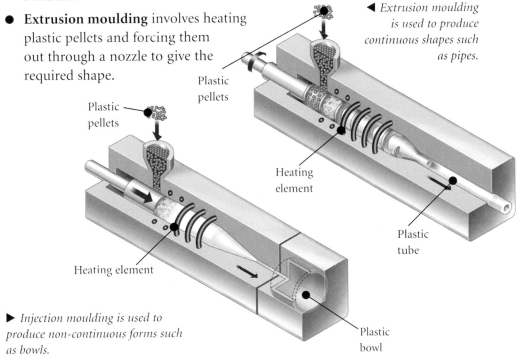

◀ *Extrusion moulding is used to produce continuous shapes such as pipes.*

Plastic pellets

Plastic pellets

Heating element

Plastic tube

Heating element

▶ *Injection moulding is used to produce non-continuous forms such as bowls.*

Plastic bowl

Radiation

- **Radiation** is an atom's way of getting rid of its excess energy.

- **There are two main kinds** of radiation: electromagnetic and particulate.

- **Electromagnetic radiation** is pure energy. It comes from electrons (see electrons).

- **Particulate radiation** is tiny bits of matter thrown out by the nuclei of atoms.

- **Particulate** radiation comes mainly from radioactive substances (see radioactivity) such as radium, uranium and other heavy elements as they break down.

- **Radiation is measured** in curies and becquerels (radiation released), röntgens (victim's exposure), rads and grays (dose absorbed), rems and sieverts (amount of radiation in the body).

- **Bacteria can stand** a radiation dose 10,000 times greater than the dose that would kill a human being.

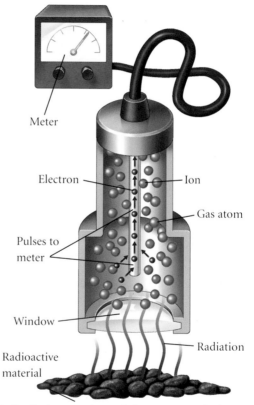

Meter

Electron

Ion

Gas atom

Pulses to meter

Window

Radiation

Radioactive material

▲ *Radiation entering a Geiger counter tube hits the gas atoms there, causing them to ionise. The electrons freed by this process spread along the wire, creating electric pulses, which are counted by a meter.*

▼ *An x-ray image made by passing electromagnetic radiation through someone's chest. It shows this person has been fitted with a pacemaker.*

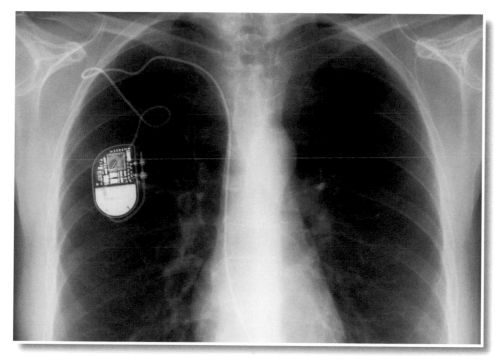

- **The Chernobyl nuclear accident** released 50 million curies of radiation. A 20 kilotonne nuclear bomb releases 10,000 times more radiation.

- **The natural radioactivity** of a brazil nut is about six becquerels (one ten-millionth of a curie), which means six atoms break up every second.

- **The natural background** radiation you receive over a year is about 100 times what you receive from a single chest x-ray.

Splitting the atom

- **In the 1890s** scientists thought that atoms were solid like billiard balls and completely unbreakable.

- **In 1897** J. J. Thomson discovered that atoms contained even smaller particles, which he called electrons (see electrons).

- **In 1900** scientists thought atoms were like plum puddings with electrons like currants on the outside.

- **In 1909** Ernest Rutherford was firing alpha particles (see radioactivity) at a sheet of gold foil. Most went straight through, but 1 in 8000 particles bounced back!

- **Rutherford concluded** that the atom was mostly empty space (which the alpha particles passed straight through) but had a tiny, dense nucleus at its centre.

- **In 1919** Rutherford managed to split the nucleus of a nitrogen atom with alpha particles. Small atoms could be split.

- **In 1932** James Chadwick found the nucleus contained two kinds of particle: protons and neutrons.

uranium atom

▲ By splitting uranium atoms, high levels of energy are produced. The atom's nucleus, which makes up almost all of its mass, is made up of protons and neutrons. These are held together by a very strong force. By harnessing this force, nuclear energy is made.

- **In 1933** Italian Enrico Fermi bombarded the big atoms of uranium with neutrons. Fermi thought the new atoms that formed had simply gained the neutrons.

- **In 1939** German scientists Hahn and Strassman repeated Fermi's experiment and found smaller atoms of barium.

- **Austrian Lise Meitner** realized that Hahn and Strassman had split the uranium atoms. This discovery opened the way to releasing nuclear energy by fission (see nuclear energy).

▲ *Ernest Rutherford put forward the idea that atoms are made up of particles of negative electricity orbiting around a heavy centre called the nucleus.*

75

Radioactivity

- **Radioactivity** is when a certain kind of atom disintegrates spontaneously and sends out little bursts of radiation from its nucleus (centre).

- **Isotopes** are slightly different versions of an atom, with either more or less neutrons (see atoms). With stable elements, such as carbon, only certain isotopes called radio-isotopes are radioactive.

- **Some large atoms,** such as radium and uranium, are so unstable that all their isotopes are radio-isotopes.

- **Radioactive isotopes** emit three kinds of radiation: alpha, beta and gamma rays.

- **When the nucleus** of an atom emits alpha or beta rays it changes and becomes the atom of a different element. This is called radioactive decay.

- **Alpha rays** are streams of alpha particles. These are made from two protons and two neutrons – basically the nucleus of a helium atom. They travel only a few centimetres and can be stopped by a sheet of paper.

- **Beta rays** are beta particles. Beta particles are electrons (or their opposite, positrons) emitted as a neutron decays into a proton. They can travel up to 1 m and can penetrate aluminium foil.

- **Gamma rays** are an energetic, short-wave form of electromagnetic radiation (see electromagnetic spectrum). They penetrate most materials but lead.

- **The half-life** of a radioactive substance is the time it takes for half its radioactive isotopes to decay. This is much easier to assess than the time for all its isotopes to decay.

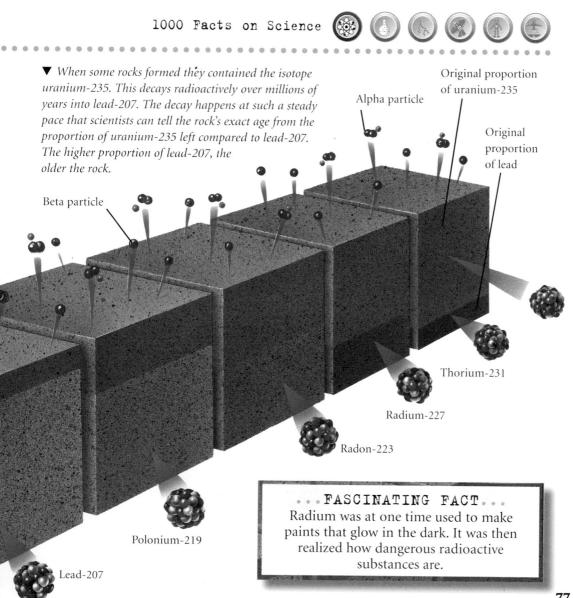

▼ *When some rocks formed they contained the isotope uranium-235. This decays radioactively over millions of years into lead-207. The decay happens at such a steady pace that scientists can tell the rock's exact age from the proportion of uranium-235 left compared to lead-207. The higher proportion of lead-207, the older the rock.*

Alpha particle

Original proportion of uranium-235

Original proportion of lead

Beta particle

Thorium-231

Radium-227

Radon-223

Polonium-219

Lead-207

...FASCINATING FACT....
Radium was at one time used to make paints that glow in the dark. It was then realized how dangerous radioactive substances are.

The Curies

- **Pierre and Marie Curie** were the husband and wife scientists who discovered the nature of radioactivity. In 1903 they won a Nobel Prize for their work.

- **Marie Curie** (1867–1934) was born Marya Sklodowska in Poland. She went to Paris in 1891 to study physics.

- **Pierre Curie** (1859–1906) was a French lecturer in physics who discovered the piezoelectric effect in crystals. His discovery led to the development of devices from quartz watches to microphones.

- **The Curies** met in 1894 while Marie was a student at the Sorbonne. They married in 1895.

- **In 1896** Antoine Becquerel found that uranium salts emitted a mysterious radiation that affected photographic paper in the same way as light.

- **In 1898** the Curies found the intensity of radiation was in exact proportion to the amount of uranium – so it must be coming from the uranium atoms.

▲ *The Curies' combination of brilliant insight with exact, patient work led to their historic breakthrough in discovering radioactivity.*

- **The Curies called** atomic radiation 'radioactivity'.

- **In July 1898** the Curies discovered a new radioactive element. Marie called it polonium after her native Poland.

- **In December** the Curies found radium – an element even more radioactive than uranium.

- **In 1906** Pierre was killed by a tram. Marie died later from the effects of her exposure to radioactive materials, the dangers of which were unknown at that time.

▲ *Marie Curie had two daughters, Irène and Ève. Throughout World War 1, Marie Curie and her daughter Irène worked on the development of using x-rays for imaging.*

Particle physics

- **Apart from the three** basic, stable particles of atoms – electrons, protons and neutrons – scientists have found over 200 rare or short-lived particles. Some were found in cosmic rays from space; some appear when atoms are smashed to bits in devices called particle accelerators.

- **Every particle** also has a mirror-image anti-particle. Although antimatter maybe much rarer, it is every bit as real.

- **Cosmic rays** contain not only electrons, protons and neutrons, but short-lived particles such as muons and strange quarks. Muons flash into existence for 2.2 micro-seconds just before the cosmic rays reach the ground.

- **Smashing atoms** in particle accelerators creates short-lived high-energy particles such as taus and pions and three kinds of quark called charm, bottom and top.

- **Particles** are now grouped into a simple framework called the Standard Model. It divides them into elementary particles and composite particles.

- **Elementary particles** are the basic particles which cannot be broken down into anything smaller. There are three groups: quarks, leptons and bosons. Leptons include electrons, muons, taus and neutrinos. Bosons are 'messenger' particles that link the others. They include photons and gluons which 'glue' quarks together.

- **Composite particles** are hadrons made of quarks glued together by gluons. They include protons, neutrons and 'hyperons' and 'resonances'.

- **To smash atoms** scientists use particle accelerators, which are giant machines set in tunnels. The accelerators use powerful magnets to accelerate particles through a tube at huge speeds, and then smash them together.

- **Huge detectors** pick up collisions between particles.

▼ *The accelerators at Fermilab near Chicago, USA, and CERN in Switzerland, are underground tubes many kilometres long through which particles are accelerated to near the speed of light.*

FASCINATING FACT
When the Fermi particle accelerator is running 250,000 particle collisions occur every second.

The particles are split up and fed towards the detector from opposite directions so they collide head-on.

Incredibly powerful electromagnets accelerate the particles.

Extra electromagnets keep the particles on track through the pipe.

Some accelerators are ring-shaped so that the particles can whizz round again and again to build up speed.

New particles are fed in from a hot filament like a giant lightbulb filament.

The detectors that record the collisions are like giant electronic cameras. They can be three storeys high and weigh over 5000 tonnes.

The pipes are heavily insulated to stop particles escaping.

81

Nuclear power

- **Nuclear power** is based on the huge amounts of energy that bind together the nucleus of every atom in the Universe. It is an incredibly concentrated form of energy.

- **Nuclear energy** is released by splitting the nuclei of atoms in a process called nuclear fission (see nuclear energy). One day scientists hope to release energy by nuclear fusion – by fusing nuclei together as in the Sun.

- **Most nuclear reactors** use uranium-235. These are special atoms, or isotopes, of uranium with 235 protons and neutrons in their nucleus rather than the normal 238.

- **The fuel** usually consists of tiny pellets of uranium dioxide in thin tubes, separated by sheets called spacers.

- **Three kilograms of uranium fuel** provide enough energy for a city of one million people for one day.

- **The earliest reactors,** called N-reactors, were designed to make plutonium for bombs. Magnox reactors make both plutonium and electricity.

- **Pressurized water reactors** (PWRs), originally used in submarines, are now the most common kind. They are built in factories, unlike Advanced Gas Reactors (AGRs).

- **Fast-breeder reactors** actually create more fuel than they burn, but the new fuel is highly radioactive.

- **Every stage of the nuclear process** creates dangerous radioactive waste. The radioactivity may take 80,000 years to fade. All but the most radioactive liquid waste is pumped out to sea. Gaseous waste is vented into the air. Solid waste is mostly stockpiled underground. Scientists debate fiercely about what to do with radioactive waste.

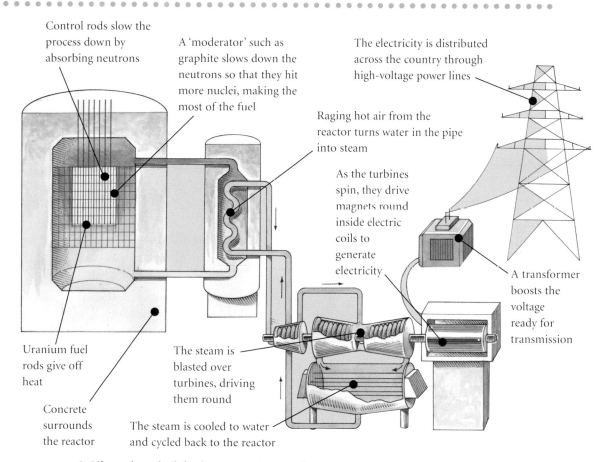

Control rods slow the process down by absorbing neutrons

A 'moderator' such as graphite slows down the neutrons so that they hit more nuclei, making the most of the fuel

The electricity is distributed across the country through high-voltage power lines

Raging hot air from the reactor turns water in the pipe into steam

As the turbines spin, they drive magnets round inside electric coils to generate electricity

A transformer boosts the voltage ready for transmission

Uranium fuel rods give off heat

Concrete surrounds the reactor

The steam is blasted over turbines, driving them round

The steam is cooled to water and cycled back to the reactor

▲ Like coal- and oil-fired power stations, nuclear power stations use steam to drive turbines to generate electricity. The difference is that nuclear power stations obtain the heat by splitting uranium atoms, not by burning coal or oil. When an atom is split, it sends out gamma rays, neutrons and immense heat. In a nuclear bomb this happens in a split second. In a nuclear power plant, control rods soak up some of the neutrons and slow the process down.

83

Nuclear energy

- **The energy** that binds the nucleus of an atom together is enormous, as Albert Einstein showed.

- **By releasing the energy** from the nuclei of millions of atoms, nuclear power stations and bombs can generate a huge amount of power.

- **Nuclear fusion** is when nuclear energy is released by fusing together small atoms such as deuterium (a kind of hydrogen).

- **Nuclear fusion** is the reaction that keeps stars glowing and gives hydrogen bombs their terrifying power.

- **Nuclear fission** releases energy by splitting the large nuclei of atoms such as uranium and plutonium.

- **To split atomic nuclei** for nuclear fission, neutrons are fired into the nuclear fuel.

- **As neutrons crash** into atoms and split their nuclei, they split off more neutrons. These neutrons bombard other nuclei, splitting off more neutrons that bombard more nuclei. This is called a chain reaction.

Neutron

Nucleus of uranium

Split nucleus

More neutrons

▶ *Nuclear fission involves firing a neutron (blue ball) into the nucleus of a uranium or plutonium atom. When the nucleus splits, it fires out more neutrons that split more nuclei, setting off a chain reaction.*

84

◀ *The huge mushroom-shaped cloud of a nuclear explosion. The four main effects from such an explosion are 1) a fireball leading to a blast wave of noise and air pressure 2) intense thermal radiation ie heat 3) initial nuclear radiation 4) residual radiation – given off later than a minute after the explosion.*

- **An atom bomb,** or A-bomb, is one of the two main kinds of nuclear weapon. It works by an explosive, unrestrained fission of uranium-235 or plutonium-239.

- **A hydrogen bomb (H-bomb)** or thermonuclear weapon uses a conventional explosion to fuse the nuclei of deuterium atoms in a gigantic nuclear explosion.

- **The H-bomb** that exploded at Novaya Zemlya in 1961 released 10,000 times more energy than the bombs dropped on Hiroshima, in Japan, in 1945.

85

Quarks

- **Quarks** are one of the three tiniest basic, or elementary, particles from which every substance is made.

- **Quarks** are too small for their size to be measured, but their mass can. The biggest quark, called a top quark, is as heavy as an atom of gold. The smallest, called an up quark, is 35,000 times lighter.

- **There are six** kinds, or flavours, of quark: up (u), down (d), bottom (b), top (t), strange (s) and charm (c).

- **Down, bottom and strange** quarks carry one-third of the negative charge of electrons; up, top and charm ones carry two-thirds of the positive charge of protons.

- **Quarks never exist** separately but in combination with one or two other quarks. Combinations of two or three quarks are called hadrons.

- **Three-quark hadrons** are called baryons and include protons and neutrons. Rare two-quark hadrons are mesons.

- **A proton** is made from two up quarks (two lots of +2/3 of a charge) and one down quark (−1/3) and has a positive charge of 1.

- **A neutron** is made from two down quarks (two lots of −1/3 of a charge) and an up quark (+2/3). The charges cancel each other out, giving a neutron no charge.

- **The theory of quarks** was first proposed by Murray Gell-Mann and Georg Zweig in 1964.

- **Quarks** are named after a famous passage in James Joyce's book *Ulysses*: 'Three quarks for Muster Mark!'

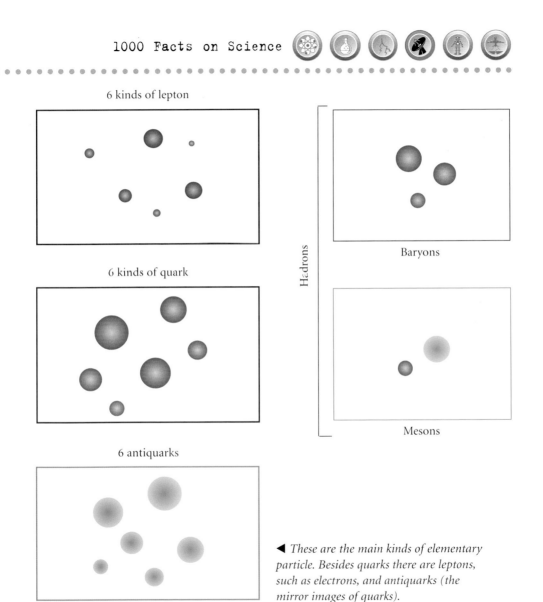

6 kinds of lepton

6 kinds of quark

6 antiquarks

Hadrons

Baryons

Mesons

◀ *These are the main kinds of elementary particle. Besides quarks there are leptons, such as electrons, and antiquarks (the mirror images of quarks).*

Spectrum

- **A spectrum** is a range of different wavelengths of electromagnetic radiation.
- **The white light of sunlight** can be broken up into its full spectrum of colours with a triangular block of glass called a prism. The prism is set in a dark room and lit only by a shaft of sunlight or similar white light.

- **The prism refracts (bends)** short wavelengths of light more than longer wavelengths, so the light fans out in bands ranging from violet to red.

- **The order of colours** in a spectrum is always the same: red, orange, yellow, green, blue, indigo, violet.

◄ *Isaac Newton first discovered that sunlight is made of all colours mixed together. It can be broken down into the seven main constituent colours since each colour has a different wavelength.*

▶ *When the beam from a torch passes through a prism it fans out into a rainbow of colours.*

- **Scientists** remember the order of the colours with the first letter of each word in this ancient phrase: 'Richard Of York Gained Battles In Vain'.

- **Infrared** is red light made of waves that are too long for human eyes to see.

- **Ultraviolet** is violet light made of waves that are too short for our eyes to see.

- **Spectroscopy,** or spectral analysis, is the study of the spectrum created when a solid, liquid or gas glows.

- **Every substance** produces its own unique spectrum, so spectroscopy helps to identify substances.

. . . **FASCINATING FACT** . . .
Spectral analysis can reveal what **anything** from a distant galaxy to a drug is made of.

Light

- **Light is a form of energy.** It is one of the forms of energy sent out by atoms when they become excited.

- **Light is just one** of the forms of electromagnetic radiation (see electromagnetic spectrum). It is the only form that we can see.

- **Although we are surrounded** by light during the day, very few things give out light. The Sun and other stars and electric lights are light sources, but we see most things only because they reflect light. If something does not send out or reflect light, we cannot see it.

▶ *This straw is not a light source, so we see it by reflected light. As the light rays reflected from the straw leave the water, they are bent, or refracted, as they emerge from the water and speed up. So the straw looks broken even though it remains intact.*

- **Light beams** are made of billions of tiny packets of energy called photons (see moving light). Together, these photons behave like waves on a pond. But the waves are tiny – 2000 would fit across a pinhead.

- **Light travels** in straight lines. The direction can be changed when light bounces off something or passes through it, but it is always straight. The straight path of light is called a ray.

- **When the path of a light ray** is blocked altogether, it forms a shadow. Most shadows have two regions: the umbra and penumbra. The umbra is the dark part where light rays are blocked altogether. The penumbra is the lighter rim where some rays reach.

- **When light rays** hit something, they bounce off, are soaked up or pass through. Anything that lets light through, such as glass, is transparent. If it mixes the light on the way through, such as frosted glass, it is translucent. If it stops light altogether, it is opaque.

- **When light strikes a surface,** some or all of it is reflected. Most surfaces scatter light in all directions, and all you see is the surface. But mirrors and other shiny surfaces reflect light in exactly the same pattern in which it arrived, so you see a mirror image.

- **When light passes** into transparent things such as water, rays are bent, or refracted. This happens because light travels more slowly in glass or water, and the rays swing round like the wheels of a car running onto sand.

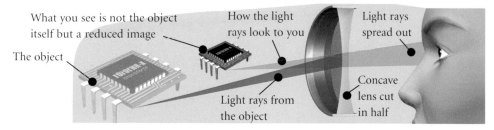

▲ *Glass lenses are shaped to refract light rays in particular ways. Concave lenses are dish-shaped lenses – thin in the middle and fat at the edges. As light rays pass through a concave lens they are bent outwards, so they spread out. The result is that when you see an object through a concave lens, it looks smaller than it really is.*

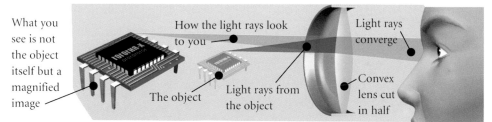

▲ *Convex lenses bulge outwards. They are fatter in the middle and thin around the edges. As light rays pass through a convex lens they are bent inwards, so they come together, or converge. When you see an object through a convex lens, it looks magnified.*

Light and atoms

- **All light comes** from atoms. They give out light when they gain energy – by absorbing light or other electromagnetic waves when hit by other particles.

- **Atoms** are normally in a 'ground' state. Their electrons circle close to the nucleus where their energy is at its lowest ebb.

- **An atom emits light** when 'excited' by taking in energy. Excitement boosts an electron's energy so it jumps further out from the nucleus.

- **An atom** only stays excited a fraction of second before the electron drops back towards the nucleus.

▲ *Spectroscopy is used to analyse the colour of light from distant stars and galaxies. It allows scientists to identify what the stars are made of.*

- **As the electron** drops back inwards, it lets go the energy it gained as a tiny packet of electromagnetic radiation called a photon.

- **Electrons** do not drop in towards the nucleus steadily like a ball rolling down a hill, but in steps, like a ball bouncing down stairs.

- **Since each step** the electron drops in has a particular energy level, so the energy of the photon depends precisely on how big the steps are. Big steps send out higher-energy short-wave photons like x-rays.

- **The colour of light** an atom sends out depends on the size of the steps its electrons jump down.

- **Each kind of atom** has its own range of electron energy steps, so each sends out particular colours of light. The range of colours each kind of atom sends out is called its emission spectrum (see spectrum). For gases, this acts like a colour signature to identify in a process called spectroscopy.

- **Just as an atom** only emits certain colours, so it can only absorb certain colours. This is its absorption spectrum.

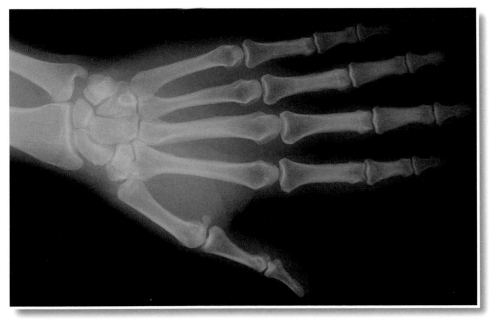

▲ *While x-rays are high-energy enough to pass through most body tissue, they cannot pass through bones. As a result, these show up as white areas on an x-ray image.*

93

Moving light

- **Light is the fastest thing** in the Universe.

- **The speed of light** is 299,792,458 metres per second.

- **Scientists remember** light's speed from the number of letters in each word of this sentence: 'We guarantee certainty, clearly referring to this light mnemonic'.

- **Isaac Newton** suggested in 1666 that light is made up of streams of tiny particles, or corpuscles.

- **The Dutch scientist** Christiaan Huygens (1629–1695) said in 1678: no, light is waves or vibrations instead.

▲ *The shimmering colours on a CD are caused by interfering light waves, where different wave lengths cancel out their peaks and troughs.*

- **In 1804 Thomas Young** showed that light is waves in a famous experiment with two narrow slits in a light beam. Light coming through each slit creates bands of shadow that must be caused by waves interfering with each other.

- **James Clerk Maxwell** suggested in the 1860s that light is electromagnetic waves.

- **Albert Einstein** showed with the photoelectric effect that light must also be particles called photons.

- **Light sometimes** looks like photons, sometimes like waves. Weirdly, in a way scientists can't explain, a single photon can interfere with itself in Young's slit experiment.

▲ *Maxwell introduced the concept of electromagnetic waves which included light, and predicted radio waves.*

> ...**FASCINATING FACT**...
> On a sunny day one thousand billion photons fall on a pinhead every second.

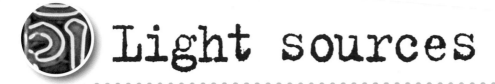

Light sources

- **Our main sources of natural light** are the Sun and the stars. The hot gases on their surface glow fiercely.

- **The brightness** of a light source is measured in candelas (cd); one candela is about as bright as a small candle.

- **For 0.1 millisecond** an atom bomb flashes out 2000 billion candelas for every square metre (m^2).

- **The Sun's surface** pumps out 23 billion candela per m^2. Laser lights are even brighter, but very small.

◀ *The fluorescent coating on the inside of a gas-filled tube produces white light when the electricity is switched on.*

- **The light falling** on a surface is measured in lux. One lux is how brightly lit something is by a light of one candela 1 m away. You need 500 lux to read by.

◀ Electrical resistance makes the thin filament in a bulb glow.

- **Electric lightbulbs** are incandescent, which means that their light comes from a thin tungsten wire, or filament, that glows when heated by an electric current.

- **Lightbulbs** are filled with an inert (unreactive) gas, such as argon, to save the filament from burning out.

- **Electric lights** were invented independently in 1878 by Englishman Sir Joseph Swan and Americans Thomas Alva Edison and Hiram Maxim.

▲ *Gas mixtures in neon lights glow different colours. Pure neon glows red.*

- **Fluorescent lights** have a glass tube coated on the inside with powders called phosphors. When electricity excites the gases in the tube to send out invisible UV rays, the rays hit the phosphors and make them glow, or fluoresce.

- **In neon lights,** a huge electric current makes the gas inside a tube electrically charged and so it glows.

Huygens

▶ *Christiaan Huygens was the leading figure of the Golden Age of Dutch science in the 17th century, making contributions in many fields.*

- **Christiaan Huygens** (1629–1695) was, after Isaac Newton, the greatest scientist of the 1600s.

- **Huygens** was born to a wealthy Dutch family in The Hague, in Holland.

- **He studied law** at the University of Leiden and the College of Orange in Breda before turning to science.

- **He worked** with his brother Constanijn to grind lenses for very powerful telescopes.

- **With his powerful telescope,** Huygens discovered in 1655 that what astronomers had thought were Saturn's 'arms' were actually rings. He made his discovery known to people in code.

- **Huygens discovered** Titan, one of Saturn's moons.

- **Huygens learned a great deal** about pendulums and built the first accurate pendulum clock.

- **Responding to Newton's theory** that light was 'corpuscles', Huygens developed the theory that light is waves (see moving light) in 1678.

- **Huygens** described light as vibrations spreading through a material called ether, which is literally everywhere and is made of tiny particles. The idea of ether was finally abandoned in the late 19th century, but not the idea of light waves.

- **Huygens' wave idea** enabled him to explain refraction (see light) simply. It also enabled him to predict correctly that light would travel more slowly in glass than in air.

▼ *Titan, Saturn's largest moon, and the only satellite in the solar system known to have clouds and a dense atmosphere, was discovered in 1655 by Christiaan Huygens.*

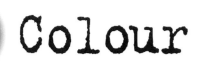

Colour

- **Colour is the way** our eyes see different wavelengths of light (see electromagnetic spectrum).

- **Red light** has the longest waves – about 700 nanometres, or nm (billionths of a metre).

- **Violet light** has the shortest waves – about 400 nm.

- **Light that is a mixture** of every colour, such as sunlight and the light from torches and ordinary lightbulbs, is called white light (see mixing colours).

- **Things are different colours** because molecules in their surface reflect and absorb certain wavelengths of light.

- **Deep-blue printers' inks** and bright-red blood are vividly coloured because both have molecules shaped like four-petalled flowers, with a metal atom at the centre.

- **Iridescence** is the shimmering rainbow colours you see flashing every now and then on a peacock's feathers, a fly's wings, oil on the water's surface or a CD.

◀ *The macaw gets its brilliant colours because pigment molecules in its feathers soak up certain wavelengths of light and reflect others, including reds, yellows and blues, very strongly.*

- **Iridescence** can be caused by the way a surface breaks the light into colours like a prism does (see spectrum).

- **Iridescence** can also be caused by interference when an object has a thin, transparent surface layer. Light waves reflected from the top surface are slightly out of step with waves reflected from the inner surface, and they interfere.

▲ *Iridescence on a CD is a result of light waves reflecting from both the top surface and the inner surface. This causes the spectrum of light which is sometimes visible.*

▲ *The surface skin of water on some spilt oil interferes with the vibrations of light causing it to be split up into the colours of the spectrum.*

> **. . . FASCINATING FACT . . .**
> As a light source gets hotter, so its colour changes from red to yellow to white to blue.

101

Mixing colours

- **White light** such as sunlight contains all the colours of the rainbow: red, orange, yellow, green, blue, indigo and violet – and all the colours in between.

- **There are three basic,** or primary colours of light – red, green and blue. They can be mixed in various proportions to make any other colour.

- **The primary colours** of light are called additive primaries, because they are added together to make different colours.

- **Each additive primary** is one third of the full spectrum of white light, so adding all three together makes white.

▲ *These circles are the primary colours of light: red, green and blue. Where two colours overlap, you see the three subtractive primaries: magenta, cyan and yellow.*

- **When two additive primaries** are added together they make a third colour, called a subtractive primary.

- **The three subtractive primaries are:** magenta (red plus blue), cyan (blue plus green) and yellow (green plus red). They too can be mixed in various proportions to make other colours.

- **Coloured surfaces** such as painted walls and pictures get their colour from the light falling on them. They soak up some colours of white light and reflect the rest. The colour you see is the colour reflected.

- **With reflected colours,** each subtractive primary soaks up one third of the spectrum of white light and reflects two-thirds of it. Mixing two subtractive primaries soaks up two-thirds of the spectrum. Mixing all three subtractive primaries soaks up all the spectrum, making black.

- **Two subtractive primaries** mixed make an additive primary.

- **Cyan and magenta** make blue; yellow and cyan make green; yellow and magenta make red.

▶ *When raindrops fall through sunlight they act as prisms. The seven main colours shine out of each raindrop in narrow bands, forming a rainbow.*

Holograms

- **Holograms** are three-dimensional photographic images made with laser lights.

- **The idea of holograms** was suggested by Hungarian-born British physicist Dennis Gabor in 1947. The idea could not be tried until laser light became available.

- **The first holograms** were made by Emmett Leith and Juris Upatnieks in Michigan, USA, in 1963 and by Yuri Denisyuk in the Soviet Union.

- **To make a hologram,** the beam from a laser light is split in two. One part of the beam is reflected off the subject onto a photographic plate. The other, called the reference beam, shines directly onto the plate.

- **The interference** between light waves in the reflected beam and light waves in the reference beam creates the hologram in complex microscopic stripes on the plate.

- **Some holograms** only show up when laser light is shone through them.

▲ *Virtual reality headsets allow the viewer to see 3-D images by showing slightly different images to each eye.*

104

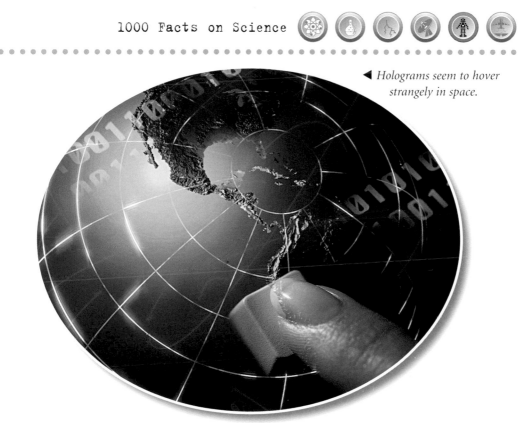

◄ *Holograms seem to hover strangely in space.*

- **Some holograms** work in ordinary light, such as those used in credit cards to stop counterfeiting.

- **Holograms** are used to detect defects in engines and aeroplanes, and forgeries in paintings by comparing two holograms made under slightly different conditions.

- **Huge amounts of digital data** can be stored in holograms in a crystal.

- **In 1993** 10,000 pages of data were stored in a lithium nobate crystal measuring just 1 cm across.

Quantum physics

- **By the 1890s** most scientists thought light moves in waves.

- **Max Planck** (1858–1947) realized that the range of radiation given out by a hot object is not quite what scientists would calculate it to be if radiation is waves.

- **Planck realized** that the radiation from a hot object could be explained if the radiation came in chunks, or quanta.

- **Quanta** are very, very small. When lots of quanta are emitted together they appear to be like smooth waves.

- **In 1905** Einstein showed that quanta explain the photoelectric effect.

- **In 1913** Niels Bohr showed how the arrangement of electrons in energy levels around an atom (see electrons) could be thought of in a quantum way too.

- **In the 1920s** Erwin Schrödinger and Werner Heisenberg developed Bohr's idea into quantum physics, a new branch of physics for particles on the scale of atoms.

▲ *Bohr was the first physicist to apply quantum theory to the problems of atomic and molecular structure.*

106

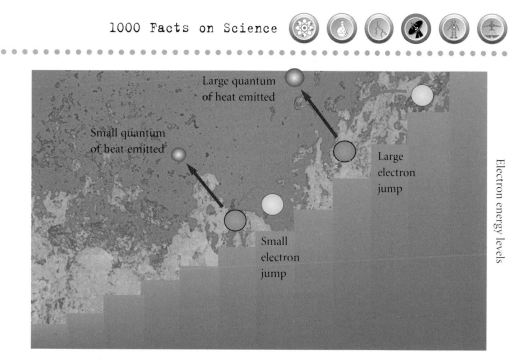

Electron energy levels

▲ *Quantum physics shows how radiation from a hot object is emitted in little chunks that are called quanta.*

- **Quantum physics** explains how electrons emit radiation (see above). It shows that an electron is both a particle and a wave, depending on how you look at it. It seems to work for all four fundamental forces (see forces) except gravity.

- **The development** of the technologies that gave us lasers and transistors came from quantum physics.

- **Quantum physics** predicts some strange things on the scale of atoms, such as particles appearing from nowhere and electrons seeming to know where each other are.

Moving particles

- **The tiny atoms and molecules** from which every substance is made are always moving.

- **The speed** at which molecules move depends on temperature.

- **Heat gives atoms and molecules** extra energy, making them move faster.

- **In 1827** Scottish botanist Robert Brown saw through a microscope that pollen grains in water were constantly dancing. They are buffeted by moving molecules that are too small to be seen. The effect is called Brownian motion.

- **In a gas,** the atoms and molecules are so far apart that they are able to zoom about freely in all directions.

▲ *As liquids boil, the atoms and molecules move around more and more energetically until some break away altogether and turn to gas. This is called evaporation.*

▼ *Air is made up of tiny, freely-moving particles. They push on any surface they come in contact with - you can see their power by looking at how they push clouds along on a windy day.*

- **Smells spread** quickly because the smell molecules move about very quickly.

- **In a liquid,** molecules are closely packed and move like dancers in a nightclub. If molecules stopped moving in liquids we would all die, because this movement is what moves materials in and out of human cells.

- **In a solid,** atoms and molecules are bound together and vibrate on the spot.

- **Air and water pressure** is simply bombardment by billions of moving molecules.

- **At −273.15°C,** which is called absolute zero, the movement of atoms and molecules slows down to a complete standstill.

Thermodynamics

- **Energy cannot be destroyed** but it can be burned up. Every time energy is used, some turns into heat. This is why you feel hot after running.

- **Energy that turns into heat** may not be lost. It dissipates (spreads out thinly in all directions) and is hard to use again.

- **Every time energy is used,** some free energy (energy available to make things happen) gets lost as heat.

- **Scientists use** the word 'entropy' to describe how much energy has become unusable. The less free energy there is, the greater the entropy.

- **The word 'entropy'** was invented by the German physicist Rudolf Clausius in 1865.

- **Clausius showed** that everything really happens because energy moves from areas of high energy to areas of low energy, from hot areas to cold areas.

- **Energy goes on flowing** from high to low until there is no difference to make anything happen. This is an equilibrium state. Entropy is the maximum.

▲ *Energy cannot be reused once it has turned to heat and dissipated, just as you cannot rebuild an igloo once the snow has melted.*

▼ *Waste gases produced from this chemical plant are burnt off and released into the atmosphere as unwanted heat.*

- **Clausius summed this idea up** in 1860s with two laws of thermodynamics.

- **The first law of thermodynamics** says the total energy in the Universe was fixed forever at the beginning of time.

- **The second law of thermodynamics** says that energy is dissipated every time it is used. So the entropy of the Universe must increase.

111

Temperature

- **Temperature** is how hot or cold something is. The best-known temperature scales are Celsius and Fahrenheit.

- **The Celsius (C) scale** is part of the metric system of measurements and is used everywhere except in the USA. It is named after Swedish astronomer Anders Celsius, who developed it in 1742.

- **Celsius is also** known as centigrade because water boils at 100°C. Cent is the Latin prefix for 100. Water freezes at 0°C.

- **On the Fahrenheit (F) scale** water boils at 212°F. It freezes at 32°F.

- **To convert Celsius** to Fahrenheit, divide by 5, multiply by 9 and add 32.

- **To convert Fahrenheit** to Celsius, subtract 32, divide by 9 and multiply by 5.

- **The Kelvin (K) scale** used by scientists is like the Celsius scale, but it begins at −273.15°C. So 0°C is 273.15K.

- **Cold:** absolute zero is −273.15°C. The coldest temperature ever obtained in a laboratory is −272.99999°C. Helium turns liquid at −269°C. Oxygen turns liquid at −183°C. Gasoline freezes at −150°C. The lowest air temperature ever recorded on Earth is −89.2°C.

◀ *A digital thermometer measures temperature with a thermistor, which is a probe whose electrical resistance varies with the heat.*

- **Hot:** the highest shade temperature recorded on Earth is 58°C. A log fire burns at around 800°C. Molten magma is about 1200°C. Tungsten melts at 3410°C. The surface of the Sun is around 6000°C. The centre of the Earth is over 7000°C. A lightning flash reaches 30,000°C. The centre of a hydrogen bomb reaches four million°C.

- **The blood temperature** of the human body is normally 37°C. A skin temperature above 40°C is very hot, and below 31°C is very cold. Hands feel cold below 20°C and go numb below 12°C. Anything above 45°C that touches your skin hurts, although people have walked on hot coals at 800°C. The knee can tolerate 47°C for 30 seconds.

▲ *Molten iron is poured into a furnace as part of the process of producing steel. The temperature of the liquid metal is about 1500°C.*

113

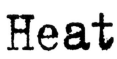

Heat

- **Heat is the energy** of moving molecules. The faster molecules move, the hotter the substance is.

- **When you hold your hand** over a heater the warmth is the assault of billions of fast-moving molecules of air.

- **Heat** is the combined energy of all the moving molecules; temperature is how fast they are moving.

▼ *Cooking helps chemical reactions to take place in food, maybe changing its flavour, its texture or consistency.*

- **The coldest temperature possible** is absolute zero, or -273°C, when molecules stop moving.

- **When you heat a substance** its temperature rises because heat makes its molecules move faster.

- **The same amount** of heat raises the temperature of different substances by different amounts.

▶ *Fire changes the energy in fuel into heat energy. Heat makes the molecules rush about.*

- **Specific heat** is the energy needed, in joules, to heat a substance by 1°C.

- **Argon gas** gets hotter quicker than oxygen. The shape of oxygen molecules means they absorb some energy not by moving faster but by spinning faster.

- **Heat always spreads out** from its source. It heats up its surroundings while cooling down itself.

...FASCINATING FACT...
Heat makes the molecules of a solid vibrate; it makes gas molecules zoom about.

115

Heat movement

- **Heat moves** in three different ways: conduction, convection and radiation.

- **Conduction** involves heat spreading from hot areas to cold areas by direct contact. It works a bit like a relay race. Energetic, rapidly moving or vibrating molecules cannon into their neighbours and set them moving.

- **Good conducting materials** such as metals feel cool to the touch because they carry heat away from your fingers quickly. The best conductors of heat are the metals silver, copper and gold, in that order.

- **Materials** that conduct heat slowly are called insulators. They help keep things warm by reducing heat loss. Wood is one of the best insulators. Water is also surprisingly effective as an insulator, which is why divers and surfers often wear wetsuits.

▲ *Hot-air balloons work because hot air is lighter than cold air and rises through it.*

◄ *A layer of water trapped between the diver and the wetsuit heats up to the person's body temperature keeping the diver warm.*

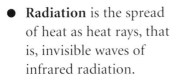
- **Radiation** is the spread of heat as heat rays, that is, invisible waves of infrared radiation.

- **Radiation** spreads heat without direct contact.

- **Convection** is when warm air rises through cool air, like a hot-air balloon.

- **Warm air rises** because warmth makes the air expand. As it expands the air becomes less dense and lighter than the cool air around it.

- **Convection currents** are circulation patterns set up as warm air (or a liquid) rises. Around the column of rising warmth, cool air continually sinks to replace it at the bottom. So the whole air turns over like a non-stop fountain.

▼ *Radioactive material causes nausea, cancer or even death and so must be guarded carefully.*

.... **FASCINATING FACT** ....
Convection currents in the air bring rain; convection currents in the Earth's interior move continents.

117

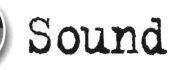

Sound

- **Most sounds** you hear, from the whisper of the wind to the roar of a jet, are simply moving air. When any sound is made it makes the air vibrate, and these vibrations carry the sound to your ears.

- **The vibrations** that carry sound through the air are called sound waves.

- **Sound waves** move by alternately squeezing air molecules together and then stretching them apart like a spring.

- **The parts of the air** that are squeezed are called condensations; the parts of the air that are stretched are called rarefactions.

- **Sound waves** travel faster through liquids and solids than through air because the molecules are more closely packed together in liquids and solids.

- **In a vacuum** such as space there is complete silence because there are no molecules to carry the sound.

▲ *When you sing, talk or shout, you are actually vibrating the vocal cords in your throat. These set up sound waves in the air you push up from your lungs.*

- **Sound travels** at about 344 m per second in air at 20°C.

- **Sound travels** faster in warm air, reaching 386 m per second at 100°C.

- **Sound travels** at 1500 m per second in pure water and at about 6000 m per second in solid steel.

- **Sound travels a million times** slower than light, which is why you hear thunder well after you see a flash of lightning, even though they both happen at the same time.

▶ *This fishing boat is using sonar to find out the depth of an object. It bounces sound waves off the object and measures how long they take to be reflected back to the boat.*

119

Sound measurement

- **The loudness of a sound** is usually measured in units called decibels (dB).

- **One decibel** is one tenth of a bel, the unit of sound named after Scots-born inventor Alexander Graham Bell.

- **Decibels** were originally used to measure sound intensity. Now they are used to compare electronic power output and voltages too.

- **Every ten points up** on the decibel scale means that a sound has increased by ten times.

- **One dB** is the smallest change the human ear can hear.

- **The quietest sound** that people can hear is 10 dB.

> ...FASCINATING FACT...
> Sounds over 130 dB are painful;
> sounds between 90–100 dB for long
> periods cause deafness.

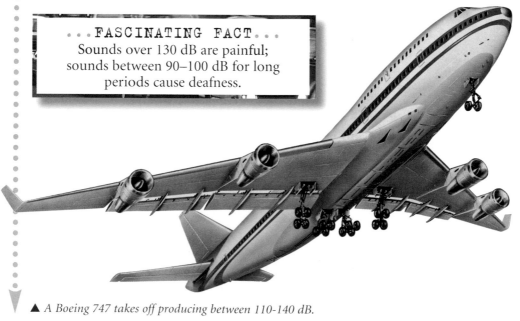

▲ A Boeing 747 takes off producing between 110-140 dB.

▲ *Heavy traffic is about 90 decibels, but it can rise higher.*

- **Quiet sounds:** a rustle of leaves or a quiet whisper is 10 dB. A quiet conversation is 30–40 dB. Loud conversation is about 60 dB. A city street is about 70 dB.

- **Loud sounds:** thunder is about 100 dB. The loudest scream ever recorded was 128.4 dB. A jet taking off is 110–140 dB. The loudest sound ever made by human technology (an atom bomb) was 210 dB.

- **The amount of energy** in a sound is measured in watts per square metre (W/m^2). Zero dB is one thousand billionths of one W/m^2.

121

Musical sound

- **Like all sounds,** musical sounds are made by something vibrating. However, the vibrations of music occur at very regular intervals.

- **The pitch** of a musical note depends on the frequency of the vibrations.

- **Sound frequency** is measured in hertz (Hz) – that is, cycles or waves per second.

- **Human ears** can hear sounds as low as about 20 Hz and up to around 20,000 Hz.

- **Middle C** on a piano measures 262 Hz. A piano has a frequency range from 27.5 to 4186 Hz.

- **The highest singing voice** can reach the E above a piano top note (4350 Hz); the lowest note is 20.6 Hz.

- **A soprano's voice** has a range from 262 to 1046 Hz; an alto from 196 to 698 Hz; a tenor from 147 to 466 Hz; a baritone from 110 to 392 Hz; a bass from 82.4 to 294 Hz.

◀ *The Italian opera singer, Luciano Pavarotti, is noted for his mastery of the highest notes of a tenor's range. He is considered one of the finest singers of recent times.*

122

- **Very few sounds** have only one pitch. Most have a fundamental (low) pitch and higher overtones.

- **The science of vibrating strings** was first worked out by Pythagoras 2500 years ago.

▼ *In most brass and woodwind instruments, such as a tuba, different frequencies are achieved by varying the length of the air column inside.*

▲ *In stringed instruments different notes – that is, different frequencies of vibrations – are achieved by varying the length of the strings.*

. . . FASCINATING FACT . . .
A song can shatter glass if the pitch of a loud note coincides with the natural frequency of vibration of the glass.

Echoes and acoustics

- **An echo** is the reflection of a sound. You hear it a little while after the sound is made.

- **You can only hear** an echo if it comes back more than 0.1 seconds after the original sound.

- **Sound travels** 34 m in 0.1 seconds, so you only hear echoes from surfaces at least 17 m away.

- **Smooth hard surfaces** give the best echoes because they break up the sound waves the least.

- **Acoustics** is the study of how sounds are created, transmitted and received.

- **The acoustics** of a space is how sound is heard and how it echoes around that space, whether it is a room or a large concert hall.

▲ *Bats emit short, high-frequency pulses of sound, inaudible to humans, and listen to the echoes returning from objects to work out their position.*

124

- **When concert halls** are designed, the idea is not to eliminate echoes altogether but to use them effectively.

- **A hall with too much echo** sounds harsh and unclear, as echoing sounds interfere with new sounds.

- **A hall without echoes** sounds muffled and lifeless.

- **Even in the best** concert halls, the music can be heard fading after the orchestra stops playing. This delay is called the reverberation time. Concert halls typically have a reverberation time of two seconds. A cathedral may reverberate for up to eight seconds, giving a more mellow, but less clear, sound.

▼ *Sydney Opera House in Australia is famous for its stunning design, but some orchestras have complained about its acoustics.*

Energy

- **Energy is the ability** to make things happen or, as scientists say, do work.

- **Energy comes in many forms,** from the chemical energy locked in sugar to the mechanical energy in a speeding train.

- **Energy does its work** either by transfer or conversion.

- **Energy transfer** is the movement of energy from one place to another, such as heat rising above a fire or a ball being thrown.

- **Energy conversion** is when energy changes from one form to another – as when wind turbines generate electric power, for instance.

- **Energy is never lost nor gained;** it simply moves or changes. The total amount of energy in the Universe has stayed the same since the dawn of time.

- **Energy and mass** are actually the same thing. They are like flip sides of a coin and are interchangeable.

- **Potential energy** is energy stored up ready for action – as in a squeezed spring or stretched piece of elastic.

▼ *Power stations do not create energy. They simply convert it into a convenient form for us to use electricity.*

- **Kinetic energy** is energy that something has because it is moving, such as a rolling ball or a falling stone.

- **Kinetic energy** increases in proportion with the velocity of an object squared. So a car has four times more kinetic energy at 40 km/h than at 20 km/h.

▼ *Found near the Earth's surface and at various depths, coal is an important primary fossil fuel.*

▼ *Wind farms may be erected in areas where there is a steady wind. About 47% of the kinetic energy of the wind can be harnessed.*

Energy conversion

- **Energy is measured** in joules (J). One joule is the energy involved in moving a force of one newton over one metre.

- **A kilojoule (kJ)** is 1000 joules.

- **A calorie** was the old measure of energy, but is now used only for food: 1 calorie is 4187 J; 1 Cal is 1000 calories.

- **For scientists,** 'work' is the transfer of energy. When-you move an object, you do work. The work done is the amount of energy (in joules) gained by the object.

▲ *A hydroelectric power station is a device that converts the energy of moving water into electrical energy.*

▼ *During sleep, the body's metabolism slows right down so that less energy is needed.*

- **For scientists, 'power'** is the work rate, or the rate at which energy is changed from one form to another.

- **The power of a machine** is the amount of work it does divided by the length of time it takes to do it.

- **The power of a car's engine** is the force with which the engine turns multiplied by the speed at which it turns.

- **A transducer** is a device for turning an electrical signal into a non-electrical signal (such as sound) or vice versa. A loudspeaker is a transducer.

- **The energy in the Big Bang** was 10^{68} J. The world's coal reserves are 2^{23} J; a thunderstorm has 1^{14} J of energy; a large egg has 400,000 J.

- **When sleeping** you use 60 Cals an hour and 80 Cals when sitting. Running uses 600 Cals. Three hours of reading or watching TV uses 240 Cals. Seven hours' hard work uses about 1000 Cals – or about 10 eggs' worth.

Engines

- **Engines are devices** that convert fuel into movement.

- **Most engines** work by burning the fuel to make gases that expand rapidly as they get hot.

- **Engines** that burn fuel to generate power are called heat engines. The burning is called combustion.

- **An internal combustion** engine, as used in a car, a jet or a rocket, burns its fuel on the inside.

- **In engines** such as those in cars and diesel trains, the hot gases swell inside a chamber (the combustion chamber) and push against a piston or turbine.

- **An external combustion** engine burns its fuel on the outside in a separate boiler that makes hot steam to drive a piston or turbine. Steam engines on trains and boats work in this way.

▲ *The Thrust car used a rocket motor to give it the acceleration it needed for its attempt on the world land speed record.*

- **Engines with pistons** that go back and forth inside cylinders are called reciprocating engines.

- **In jets and rockets,** hot gases swell and push against the engine as they shoot out of the back.

- **In four-stroke engines,** such as those in most cars, the pistons go up and down four times for each time they are thrust down by the hot gases.

- **In two-stroke engines,** such as those on small motorcycles, lawnmowers and chainsaws, the piston is pushed by burning gases every time it goes down.

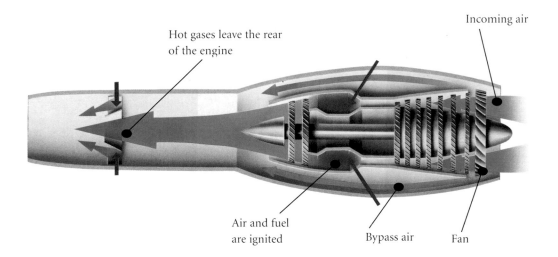

Incoming air

Hot gases leave the rear
of the engine

Air and fuel
are ignited

Bypass air

Fan

▲ *A jet engine burns fuel with air drawn in from the atmosphere in order to generate gases: it discharges these from the rear to power the craft along.*

Inertia and momentum

- **Everything that is standing still** has inertia, which means that it will not move unless forced to.

- **Everything that moves** has momentum, which means that it will not slow down or speed up or change direction unless forced to.

- **There is no real difference** between inertia and momentum, because everything in the Universe is moving. Things only appear to be still because they are not moving relative to something else.

▲ *The lead shot that athletes throw when they put the shot has a large mass. It takes a lot of muscle power to overcome its inertia.*

- **An object's momentum** is its mass times its velocity.

- **Something heavy** or fast has a lot of momentum, so a large force is needed to slow it down or speed it up.

- **A ball moves** when you kick it because when a moving object strikes another, its momentum is transferred. This is the law of conservation of momentum.

- **Angular momentum** is the momentum of something spinning. It depends on its speed and the size of the circle.

- **When a spinning skater** draws his arms close to his body, the circle he is making is smaller yet his angular momentum must be the same. So he spins faster.

- **For the same reason**, a satellite orbiting close to the Earth travels faster than one orbiting farther out.

- **A spinning top stays** upright because its angular momentum is greater than the pull of gravity.

▶ *If a spinning top is given a knock it will go round at a slant. If spun with a slant at the start, it will quickly right itself until halted by friction.*

133

Motion

- **Every movement** in the Universe is governed by physical laws devised by people such as Newton and Einstein.

- **Newton's first law of motion** says an object accelerates, slows down or changes direction only when a force is applied.

- **Newton's second law of motion** says that the acceleration depends on how heavy the object is, and on how hard it is being pushed or pulled.

- **The greater the force** acting on an object, the more it will accelerate.

- **The heavier an object is** – the greater its mass – the less it will be accelerated by a particular force.

- **Newton's third law of motion** says that when a force pushes or acts one way, an equal force pushes in the opposite direction.

- **Newton's third law of motion** is summarized as follows: 'To every action, there is an equal and opposite reaction'.

◀ *To start moving, a skater uses the force of his muscles to push against the ground. As he or she pushes, the ground pushes back with equal force.*

▲ *During launch, the blast of gases shooting from the rear of the shuttle produces 31,000,000 newtons of thrust, enough to allow it to break through the force of gravity.*

- **Newton's third law** applies everywhere, but you can see it in effect in a rocket in space. In space there is nothing for the rocket to push on. The rocket is propelled by the action and reaction between the hot gases pushed out by its engine and the rocket itself.

- **You cannot always see** the reaction. When you bounce a ball on the ground, it looks as if only the ball bounces, but the Earth recoils too. The Earth's mass is so great compared to the ball's that the recoil is tiny.

- **Einstein's theory** of relativity modifies Newton's second law of motion under certain circumstances.

135

Velocity and acceleration

- **Velocity** is speed in a particular direction.
- **Uniform velocity** is when the velocity stays the same. It can be worked out simply by dividing the distance travelled (d) by the time (t): $v = d/t$.
- **Acceleration** is a change in velocity.
- **Positive acceleration** is getting faster; negative acceleration is getting slower.
- **Acceleration** is typically given in metres per second per second, or m/s^2. This means that in each second, a velocity gets faster by so many metres per second per second.

▲ *A motorbike accelerates much faster than a car because of its power-to-weight ratio.*

▲ *For a brief moment as they come away from the start, sprinters accelerate faster than a Ferrari car.*

- **A rifle bullet** accelerates down the barrel at 3000 m/s². A fast car accelerates at 6 m/s².

- **When an object falls,** the Earth's gravity makes it accelerate at 9.81 m/s². This is called g.

- **Acceleration** is often described in gs.

- **In a rocket taking off** at 1 g, the acceleration has little effect. But at 3 g, it is impossible to move your arms and legs; at 4.5 g you would black out in five seconds.

- **A high-speed lift** goes up at 0.2 g. An aeroplane takes off at 0.5 g. A car brakes at up to 0.7 g. In a crash, you may be able to survive a momentary deceleration of up to 100 g, but the effects are likely to be severe.

137

Newton

- **Sir Isaac Newton** was one of the greatest scientists. His book *The Mathematical Principles of Natural Philosophy* is the most influential science book ever written.

- **Newton was born** on December 25, 1642 in Woolsthorpe in Lincoln, England. As a boy, he often made mechanical devices such as model windmills and water clocks.

- **With his theory of gravity** Newton discovered how the Universe is held together.

- **Newton** said that his theory of gravity was inspired by seeing an apple fall from a tree when he left Cambridge to escape the plague.

▲ *Newton invented a kind of telescope that is now standard for astronomers.*

- **Newton invented** an entirely new branch of mathematics called calculus. Independently, Leibniz also invented it.

- **Newton** discovered that sunlight is a mixture of all colours (see spectrum).

- **The interference** patterns from reflected surfaces (like a pool of oil) are called Newton's rings.

- **Newton** spent much of his life studying astrology and alchemy.

- **Newton never married** and at times was almost a recluse. Shortly before he died in 1727 he said: 'I seem to have been only like a boy playing on the seashore, and diverting myself in now and then finding a smoother pebble or prettier shell than ordinary, whilst the great ocean of truth lay all undiscovered before me.'

- **Newton** was a Member of Parliament, president of the Royal Society and master of the Royal Mint, where he found a way to make coins more accurately.

▲ *A telescope in an optical observatory stands under a large dome that has shutters. Observatories use two main kinds of telescope. Reflecting (Newtonian) telescopes use a curved mirror or set of such mirrors to focus light, and refracting telescopes use a system of lenses.*

Machines

- **A machine** is a device that makes doing work easier by reducing the effort needed to move something.

- **There are two forces** involved in every machine: the Load that the machine has to overcome, and the effort used to move the load.

- **The amount that a machine** reduces the effort needed to move a load is called the Mechanical Advantage. This tells you how effective a machine is.

- **Basic machines include** levers, gears, pulleys, screws, wedges and wheels. More elaborate machines, such as cranes, are built up from combinations of these basic machines.

- **Machines cut** the effort needed to move a load by spreading the effort over a greater distance or time.

- **The distance** moved by the effort you apply, divided by the distance moved by the load, is called the Velocity Ratio (VR).

- **If the VR is greater** than 1, then the Effort moves farther than the Load. You need less effort to move the load, but you have to apply the effort for longer.

- **The total amount** of effort you use to move something is called Work. Work is the force you apply multiplied by the distance that the load moves.

▲ *Like many aspects of modern life, farming has become increasingly dependent on the use of machines.*

- **One of the earliest machine still used today** is a screw-like water-lifting device called a dalu, first used in Sumeria 5500 years ago.

- **One of the world's biggest machines** is the SMEC earthmover used in opencast mines in Australia. It weighs 180 tonnes and has wheels 3.5 m high.

▼ *Excavators like this can do the work of many people and is a common sight on construction sites.*

Forces

- **A force** is a push or a pull. It can make something start to move, slow down or speed up, change direction or change shape or size. The greater a force, the more effect it has.

- **The wind is a force.** Biting, twisting, stretching, lifting and many other actions are also forces. Every time something happens, a force is involved.

- **Force is measured** in newtons (N). One newton is the force needed to speed up a mass of one kilogram by one metre per second every second.

- **When something moves** there are usually several forces involved. When you throw a ball, the force of your throw hurls it forwards, the force of gravity pulls it down and the force of air resistance slows it down.

- **The direction and speed** of movement depend on the combined effect of all the forces involved – this is called the resultant.

- **A force** has magnitude (size) and works in a particular direction.

- **A force can** be drawn on a diagram as an arrow called a vector (see vectors). The arrow's direction shows the force's direction. Its length shows the force's strength.

▶ *When a spacecraft lifts off, the force of the rocket has to overcome the forces of gravity and air resistance to power the craft upwards.*

- **Four fundamental forces** operate throughout the Universe: gravity, electric and magnetic forces (together called electromagnetic force), and strong and weak nuclear forces (see nuclear energy).

- **A force field** is the area over which a force has an effect. The field is strongest closest to the source and gets weaker farther away.

▲ *The force of the sea's waves is unpredictable. One day huge waves may crash down, on others the sea may be absolutely calm.*

...FASCINATING FACT...
The thrust of Saturn V's rocket engines
was 33 million newtons.

Vectors

- **For scientists,** vectors are things that have both a particular size and a particular direction.

- **Forces** such as gravity, muscles or the wind are vector quantities.

- **Acceleration** is a vector quantity.

- **Scalar quantities** are things which have a particular size but have no particular direction.

- **Speed, density and mass** are all scalar quantities.

- **Velocity** is speed in a particular direction, so it is a vector quantity.

- **A vector** can be drawn on a diagram with an arrow that is proportional in length to its size, pointing in the right direction.

- **Several vectors** may affect something at the same time. As you sit on a chair, gravity pulls you downwards while the chair pushes you up, so you stay still. But if someone pushes the chair from behind, you may tip over. The combined effect of all the forces involved is called the resultant.

- **When several vectors** affect the same thing, they may act at different angles. You can work out their combined effect – the resultant – by drawing geometric diagrams with the vectors.

▲ *As a gymnast poses in mid-routine, she unconsciously combines the forces acting on her to keep her in balance. These forces, such as her weight and forward momentum, are all vectors and could be worked out geometrically on paper.*

- **The parallelogram of forces** is a simple geometric diagram for working out the resultant from two forces. A vector arrow is drawn for each force from the same point. A parallel arrow is then drawn from the end of each arrow to make a parallelogram. The resultant is the simple diagonal of the parallelogram.

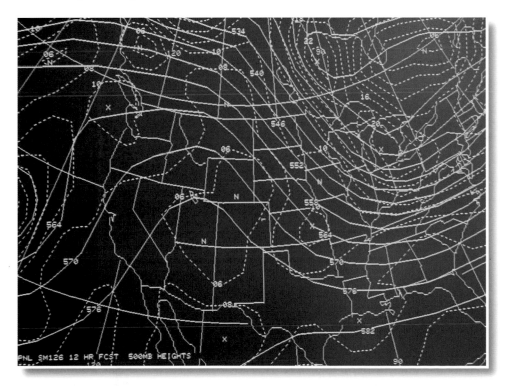

▲ *Various types of maps and charts are used to predict the weather. Vector maps are useful since they describe both speed and direction – invaluable for depicting the course of winds or storms.*

Turning forces

- **Every force** acts in a straight line. Things move round because of a 'turning effect'.

- **A turning effect** is a force applied to an object that is fixed or pivots in another place, called the fulcrum.

- **In a door** the fulcrum is the hinge.

- **The size of a turning force** is known as the moment.

- **The farther from the fulcrum** that a force is applied, the bigger the moment is.

- **A lever** makes it much easier to move a load by making use of the moment (size of turning force).

- **A first-class lever,** such as pliers or scissors, has the fulcrum between the effort and the load; a second-class lever, such as a screwdriver or wheelbarrow, has the load between the effort and the fulcrum; a third-class lever, such as your lower arm or tweezers, has the effort between the load and the fulcrum.

Load

Fulcrum

Effort

◄ *A pair of scissors is really two knife blades joined together to form a double lever. Each blade operates as a first-class lever.*

146

- **Gears are sets of wheels** of different sizes that turn together. They make it easier to cycle uphill, or for a car to accelerate from a standstill, by spreading the effort over a greater distance.

- **The gear ratio** is the number of times that the wheel doing the driving turns the wheel being driven.

- **The larger the gear ratio** the more the turning force is increased, but the slower the driven wheel turns.

Fulcrum (elbow)

Effort (where the muscle joins the bone)

▶ *The human lower arm is an example of a third-class lever. The effort is between the fulcrum and the load.*

Load (in the hand)

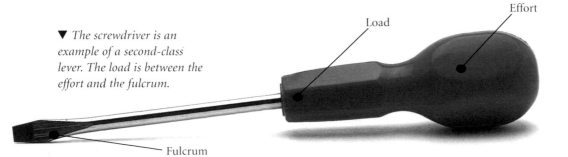

▼ *The screwdriver is an example of a second-class lever. The load is between the effort and the fulcrum.*

Load

Effort

Fulcrum

147

Stretching and pulling

- Elasticity is the ability of a solid material to return to its original shape after it has been misshapen.

- A force that misshapes material is called a stress.

- All solids are slightly elastic but some are very elastic, for example rubber, thin steel and young skin.

- Solids return to their original shape after the stress stops, as long as the stress is less than their 'elastic limit'.

- Strain is how much a solid is stretched or squeezed when under stress, namely how much longer it grows.

- The amount a solid stretches under a particular force – the ratio of stress to strain – is called the elastic modulus, or Young's modulus.

▶ *A bungee jumper stretches a piece of elasticated rope to a great extent. The rope then returns to its original length pulling the jumper back in the air.*

...**FASCINATING FACT**...
Some types of rubber can be stretched
1000 times beyond its original length
before it reaches its elastic limit.

- The greater the stress, the greater the strain. This is called Hooke's law, after Robert Hooke (1635–1703).

- Solids with a low elastic modulus, such as rubber, are stretchier than ones with a high modulus, such as steel.

- Steel can be only stretched by 1% before it reaches its elastic limit. If the steel is coiled into a spring, this 1% can allow a huge amount of stretching and squeezing.

▲ *The leverage of the bow string helps an archer to bend the elastic material of the bow so far that it has tremendous power as it snaps back into shape.*

Weight and mass

- **Mass** is the amount of matter in an object.

- **Weight** is not the same as mass. Scientists say weight is the force of gravity pulling on an object. Weight varies with the mass of the object and the strength of gravity.

- **Objects weigh more** at sea level, which is nearer the centre of the Earth, than up a mountain.

- **A person on the Moon** weighs one sixth of their weight on Earth because the Moon's gravity is one sixth of the Earth's gravity.

- **Weight varies** with gravity but mass is always the same, so scientists use mass when talking about how heavy something is.

- **The smallest** known mass is that of a photon (see light and atoms). Its mass is 5.3 times 10^{-63} (62 zeros and a 1 after the decimal point) kg.

- **The mass of the Earth** is 6×10^{24} (six trillion trillion) kg. The mass of the Universe may be 10^{51} (10 followed by 50 zeros) kg.

- **Density is** the amount of mass in a certain space. It is measured in grams per cubic centimetre (g/cm^3).

- **The lightest** solids are silica aerogels made for space science, with a density of 0.005 g/cm^3. The lightest gas is hydrogen, at 0.00008989 g/cm^3. The density of air is 0.00128 g/cm^3.

- **The densest** solid is osmium at 22.59 g/cm^3. Lead is 11.37 g/cm^3. A neutron star has an incredible density of about one billion trillion g/cm^3.

▲ *Brass weights are used in chemical laboratories because brass is dense and does not corrode.*

▲ *The pull of gravity at the Moon's surface is only one sixth as strong as on Earth.*

151

Floating and sinking

- **Things float** because they are less dense in water, which is why you can lift quite a heavy person in a swimming pool. This loss of weight is called buoyancy.

- **Buoyancy** is created by the upward push, or upthrust, of the water.

- **When an object** is immersed in water, its weight pushes it down. At the same time the water pushes it back up with a force equal to the weight of water displaced (pushed out of the way). This is called Archimedes' principle (see Archimedes).

- **An object sinks** until its weight is exactly equal to the upthrust of the water, at which point it floats.

- **Things that are less dense** than water float; those that are more dense sink.

- **Steel ships** float because although steel is denser than water, their hulls are full of air. They sink until enough water is displaced to match the weight of steel and air in the hull.

- **Oil floats** on water because it is less dense.

▲ A fishing float is made of a buoyant material such as cork or plastic in order to hold the bait suspended in the water. It bobs when a fish bites the hook.

- **Ships float** at different heights according to how heavily laden they are and how dense the water is.

- **Ships float higher** in sea water than in fresh water because salt makes the sea water more dense.

- **Ships float higher** in dense cold seas than in warm tropical ones. They float higher in the winter months.

▲ *The liner* Titanic *was said to be unsinkable. However, as soon as an iceberg breached its hull and let in water to replace the air, it sank like a stone.*

153

Friction

- **Friction** is the force that acts between two things rubbing together. It stops them sliding past each other.

- **The friction** that stops things starting to slide is called static friction. The friction that slows down sliding surfaces is called dynamic friction.

- **The harder** two surfaces are pressed together, the greater the force that is needed to overcome friction.

- **The coefficient of friction** (**CF**) is the ratio of the friction to the weight of the sliding object.

▲ *This car is streamlined to reduce drag (friction with air). The air flows over and under its 'wing', producing a downward force that presses the car to the ground, enabling it to go faster.*

▲ *Waxed skis on snow have a CF of just 0.14, allowing cross-country skiers to slide along the ground very easily.*

- **Metal sliding on metal** has a CF of 0.74; ice sliding on ice has a CF of 0.1. This means it is over seven times harder to make metal slide on metal than ice on ice.

- **Friction often makes things hot.** As the sliding object is slowed down, much of the energy of its momentum is turned into heat.

- **Fluid friction** is the friction between moving fluids or between a fluid and a solid. It is what makes thick fluids viscous (less runny).

- **Oil reduces friction** by creating a film that keeps the solid surfaces apart.

- **Brakes use dynamic friction** to slow things down.

- **Drag is friction** between air and an object. It slows a fast car, or any aircraft moving through the air.

Pressure

- **Pressure** is the force created by the assault of fast-moving molecules.

- **The pressure that keeps** a bicycle tyre inflated is the constant assault of huge numbers of air molecules on the inside of the tyre.

- **The water pressure that** crushes a submarine when it dives too deep is the assault of huge numbers of water molecules.

▼ *The worst storms, such as this hurricane seen from space, are caused when air from high-pressure areas rushes into low-pressure areas.*

- **Pressure rises** as you go deeper in the ocean. This is because the water becomes denser and denser and the number of water molecules increases.

- **The water pressure 10,000 m** below the surface is equivalent to seven elephants standing on a dinner plate.

- **The pressure of the air** on the outside of your body is balanced by the pressure of fluids inside. Without this internal pressure, air pressure would crush your body instantly.

- **Pressure** is measured as the force on a certain area.

- **The standard unit** of pressure is a pascal (Pa) or 1 newton per sq m (N/m^2).

- **High pressures:** the centre of the Earth may be 400 billion Pa; steel can withstand 40 million Pa; a shark bite can be 30 million Pa.

- **Low pressures:** the best laboratory vacuum is 1 trillionth Pa; the quietest sound is 200 millionths Pa. The pressure of sunlight may be 3 millionths Pa.

▲ *A submarine is protected by two hulls. The inner of these is built of thick, strong steel, and is called the pressure hull. It shields the ship from the crushing force of the water.*

157

Archimedes

- **Archimedes** (c.287–212BC) was one of the first great scientists. He created the sciences of mechanics and hydrostatics.

- **Archimedes** was a Greek who lived in the city of Syracuse, Sicily. His relative, Hieron II, was king of Syracuse.

- **Archimedes' screw** is a simple pump supposedly invented by Archimedes. It scoops up water with a spiral device that turns inside a tube. It is still used in the Middle East.

- **To help defend** Syracuse against Roman attackers in 215BC, Archimedes invented many war machines. They included an awesome 'claw' – a giant grappling crane that could lift whole galleys from the water and sink them.

- **Archimedes** was killed by Roman soldiers when collaborators let the Romans into Syracuse in 212BC.

- **Archimedes** analysed levers mathematically. He showed that the load you can move with a particular effort is in exact proportion to its distance from the fulcrum.

- **Archimedes discovered** that things float because they are thrust upwards by the water.

- **Archimedes' principle** shows that the upthrust on a floating object is equal to the weight of the water that the object pushes out of the way.

- **Archimedes** realized he could work out the density, or specific gravity, of an object by comparing the object's weight to the weight of water it pushes out of a jar when completely submerged.

- **Archimedes** used specific gravity to prove a sly goldsmith had not made King Hieron's crown of pure gold.

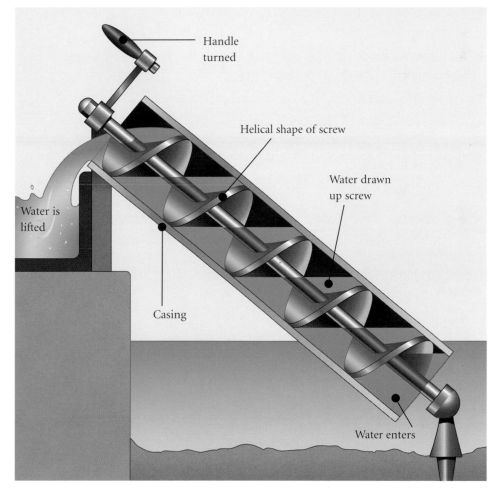

Handle
turned

Helical shape of screw

Water drawn
up screw

Water is
lifted

Casing

Water enters

▲ *The Archimedes' screw draws up water by turns of a long screw held inside a tightly fitting cylinder. The casing fits snugly to stop any leakage.*

159

Magnetism

- **Magnetism** is the invisible force between materials such as iron and nickel. Magnetism attracts or repels.

- **A magnetic field** is the area around a magnet inside which its magnetic force can be detected.

- **An electric current** creates its own magnetic field.

- **A magnet** has two poles: a north pole and a south pole.

- **Like (similar) poles** (e.g. two north poles) repel each other; unlike poles attract each other.

- **The Earth** has a magnetic field that is created by electric currents inside its iron core. The magnetic north pole is close to the geographic North Pole.

- **If left to swivel freely,** a magnet will turn so that its north pole points to the Earth's magnetic north pole.

- **The strength of a magnet** is measured in teslas. The Earth's magnetic field is 0.00005 teslas.

- **All magnetic materials** are made up of tiny groups of atoms called domains. Each one is like a mini-magnet with north and south poles. When material is magnetized, millions of domains line up.

...FASCINATING FACT...
One of the world's strongest magnets is at the Lawrence Berkeley National Laboratory, California, USA. Its field is 250,000 times stronger than the Earth's.

▶ *Some animals seem to detect the Earth's magnetic field and use it to help them find their way when they migrate. Birds which have this built-in compass include swallows, geese and pigeons.*

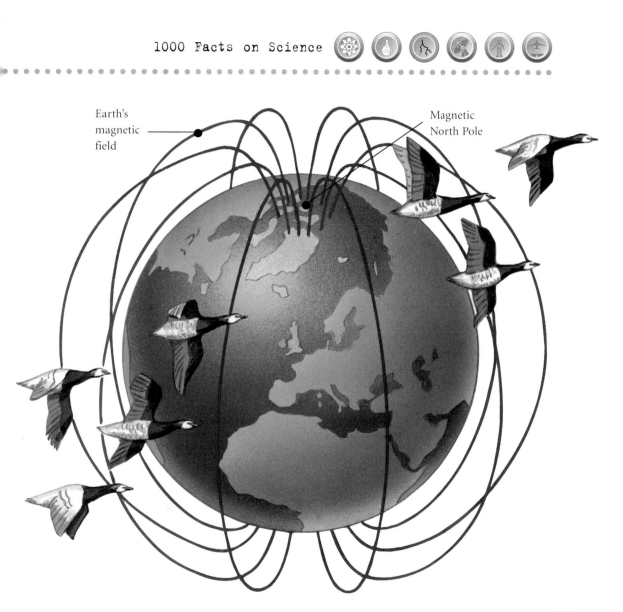

Earth's magnetic field

Magnetic North Pole

Electricity

- **Electricity** is the energy that makes everything from toasters to televisions work. It is also linked to magnetism. Together, as electromagnetism, they are one of the four fundamental forces holding the Universe together.

- **Electricity** is made by tiny bits of atoms called electrons. Electrons have an electrical charge which is a force that either pulls bits of atoms together or pushes them apart.

- **Some particles** (bit of atoms) have a negative electrical charge; others have a positive charge.

- **Particles** with the same charge push each other away. Particles with the opposite charge pull together.

▲ *Try making your own static electricity. Comb your hair quickly, if possible on a cold, dry day, and watch how it stands up.*

- **Electrons** have a negative electrical charge.

- **There are the same number** of positive and negative particles in most atoms so the charges usually balance out.

- **Electricity** is created when electrons move, building up negative charge in one place, or carrying it along.

- **Static electricity** is when the negative charge stays in one place. Current electricity is when the charge moves.

- **Electric charge** is measured with an electroscope.

- **Materials** that let electrons (and electrical charge) move through them easily, such as copper, are called conductors. Materials that stop electrons passing through, such as rubber, are called insulators.

▲ *Lightning is one of the most dramatic displays of natural electricity.*

163

Electric power

- **Most electricity is generated in power stations** by magnets that spin between coils of wire to induce an electric current (see electric circuits).

- **The magnets** are turned by turbines, which are themselves either turned by steam heated by burning coal, oil or gas, or by nuclear fuel, or turned by wind or water.

- **The stronger the magnet,** the faster it turns, the more coils there are, so the bigger the voltage created.

- **Simple dynamos** generate a direct current (DC) that always flows in the same direction.

- **The generators** in power stations are alternators that give an alternating current (AC) which continually swaps direction. In an alternator, as the magnets spin they pass the wires going up on one side and down on the other.

- **The system of power transmission** that takes electricity into homes was developed by Croatian-born US engineer Nikola Tesla at Niagara, USA in the 1880s.

- **Electricity from power stations** is distributed around a country in a network of cables known as the grid.

- **Power station** generators push out 25,000 volts or more. This voltage is too much to use in people's homes, but not enough to transmit over long distances.

- **To transmit** electricity over long distances, the voltage is boosted to 400,000 volts by step-up transformers. It is fed through high-voltage cables. Near its destination the electricity's voltage is reduced by step-down transformers at substations for distribution to homes, shops, offices and factories.

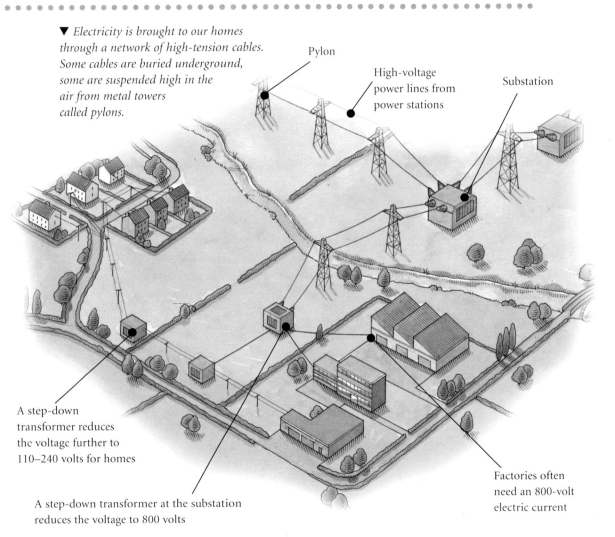

▼ *Electricity is brought to our homes through a network of high-tension cables. Some cables are buried underground, some are suspended high in the air from metal towers called pylons.*

Pylon

High-voltage power lines from power stations

Substation

A step-down transformer reduces the voltage further to 110–240 volts for homes

A step-down transformer at the substation reduces the voltage to 800 volts

Factories often need an 800-volt electric current

165

Electric circuits

- **An electric charge** that does not move is called static electricity (see electricity). A charge may flow in a current providing there is an unbroken loop, or circuit.

- **A current only flows** through a good conductor such as copper, namely a material that transmits charge well.

- **A current only flows** if there is a driving force to push the charge. This force is called an electromotive force (emf).

- **The emf** is created by a battery or a generator.

- **Currents were once thought to** flow like water. In fact they move like a row of marbles knocking into each other.

- **In a good conductor** there are lots of free electrons that are unattached to atoms. These are the 'marbles'.

- **A current only flows** if there are more electrons at one point in the circuit. This difference, called the potential difference, is measured in volts.

- **The rate at which current** flows is measured in amps. It depends on the voltage and the resistance (how much the circuit obstructs the flow of current). Resistance is measured in ohms.

Spring

Batteries

Switch

Metal strip

Light bulb

▶ *A metal strip, moved by the torch's switch, connects the current from the batteries to the light bulb.*

● **Batteries** give out Direct Current (DC), a current that flows in one direction. Power stations send out Alternating Current (AC), which swaps direction 50–60 times per second.

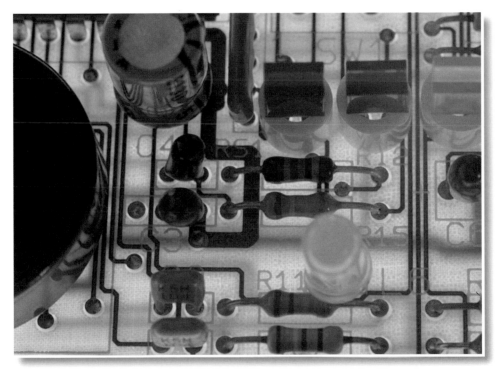

▲ *Resistors, transistors, capacitors and diodes are the main components of a circuit board.*

. . . **FASCINATING FACT** . . .
The electrical resistance of dry skin is 500,000 ohms; wet skin's is just 1000 ohms.

Electronics

- **Electronics** are the basis of many modern technologies, from hi-fi systems to missile control systems.

- **Electronics** are systems that control things by automatically switching tiny electrical circuits on and off.

- **Transistors** are electronic switches. They are made of materials called semiconductors that change their ability to conduct electricity.

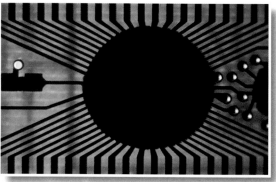
▼ *Microprocessors contain millions of transistors in a package that is no bigger than a human fingernail.*

- **Electronic systems work** by linking many transistors together so that each controls the way the others work.

- **Diodes** are transistors with two connectors. They control an electric current by switching it on or off.

- **Triodes** are transistors with three connectors that amplify the electric current (make it bigger) or reduce it.

- **A silicon chip** is thousands of transistors linked together by thin metal strips in an integrated circuit, on a single crystal of the semi-conductor, silicon.

- **The electronic areas** of a chip are those treated with traces of chemicals such as boron and phosphorus, which alter the conductivity of silicon.

- **Microprocessors** are complete Central Processing Units (see computers) on a single silicon chip.

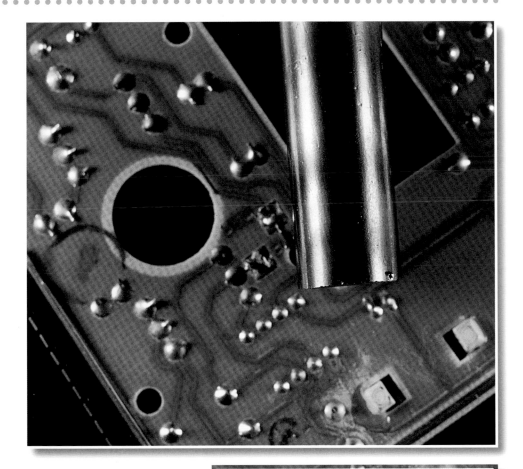

▲ *The components on silicon chips are so minute that photographing them involves using a microscope.*

...**FASCINATING FACT**...
Some microprocessors can now handle billions of bits of data every second.

Faraday

- **Michael Faraday** (1791–1867) was one of the greatest scientists of the 19th century.

- **Faraday was the son** of a poor blacksmith, born in the village of Newington in Surrey, England.

- **He started work as** an apprentice bookbinder but became assistant to the great scientist Humphry Davy after taking brilliant notes at one of Davy's lectures.

- **Faraday was said** to be Davy's greatest discovery.

- **Until 1830 Faraday** was mainly a chemist. In 1825 he discovered the important chemical benzene.

▲ *Faraday drew huge crowds to his brilliant and entertaining Christmas lectures on science at the Royal Institution in London. These Christmas lectures at the Royal Institution continue to be a popular tradition today.*

- **In 1821** Faraday showed that the magnetism created by an electric current would make a magnet move and so made a very simple version of an electric motor.

- **In 1831** Faraday showed that when a magnet moves close to an electric wire, it creates, or induces, an electric current in the wire. This was discovered at the same time by Joseph Henry in the USA.

- **Using** his discovery of electric induction, Faraday made the first dynamo to generate electricity and so opened the way to the modern age of electricity.

- **In the 1840s** Faraday suggested the idea of lines of magnetic force and electromagnetic fields. These ideas, which were later developed by James Clerk Maxwell, underpin much of modern science.

- **Faraday** was probably the greatest scientific experimenter of all time.

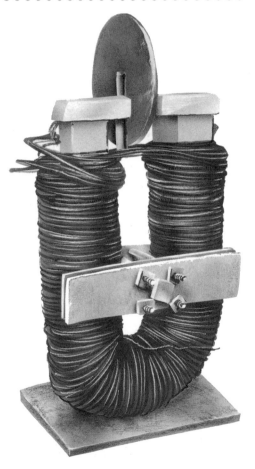

▲ *Faraday's disc generator. An electromotive force (emf) is produced in a copper disc when it is spun in the magnetic field lying between the poles of an electromagnet.*

171

Electromagnetism

- **Electromagnetism** is the combined effect of electricity and magnetism.

- **Every electric current** creates its own magnetic field.

- **Maxwell's screw rule** says that the magnetic field runs the same way a screw turns if you screw it in the direction of the electric current.

- **An electromagnet** is a strong magnet that is only magnetic when an electric current passes through it. It is made by wrapping a coil of wire, called a solenoid, around a core of iron.

- **Electromagnets** are used in everything from ticket machines and telephones to loudspeakers.

- **Magnetic levitation** trains use very strong electromagnets to carry the train on a cushion of magnetic repulsion.

- **When an electric wire** is moved across a magnetic field, an electric current is created, or induced, in the wire. This is the basis of every kind of electricity generation.

◀ *Wind turbines generate electricity by using the wind to turn their blades. These drive magnets around inside coils of electric wire.*

▶ *Maglev trains are suspended by powerful magnets above a guide track. Early versions were built in Germany and Japan, and in 1996 a Maglev train started operating at Disney World in Florida, USA, running at speeds of more than 400 km/h.*

- **Fleming's right-hand rule** says that if you hold your right thumb, first and middle fingers at 90° to each other, your middle finger shows the direction of the induced current – if your thumb points in the direction the wire moves and your first finger points out the magnetic field.

- **Electromagnetism** can be switched on and off, unlike permanent magnets.

- **Around every** electric or magnetic object is an area, or electromagnetic field, where its force is effective.

Electromagnetic spectrum

- **The electromagnetic spectrum** is the complete range of radiation sent out by electrons (see light and atoms). It is given off in tiny packages of energy called photons, which can be either particles or waves (see moving light).

- **Electromagnetic waves** vary in length and frequency. The shorter the wave, the higher its frequency (and also its energy).

- **The longest waves** are over 100 kilometres long; the shortest are less than a billionth of a millimetre long.

- **All electromagnetic waves** travel at 300,000 kilometres per second, which is the speed of light.

- **Visible light** is just a small part of the spectrum.

- **Radio waves,** including microwaves and television waves, and infrared light, are made from waves that are too long for human eyes to see.

- **Long waves** are lower in energy than short waves. Long waves from space penetrate the Earth's atmosphere easily (but not solids, like short waves).

- **Ultraviolet light,** x-rays and gamma rays are made from waves that are too short for human eyes to see.

- **Short waves are very energetic.** But short waves from space are blocked out by Earth's atmosphere – which is fortunate because they are dangerous. x-rays and gamma rays penetrate some solids, and UV rays can penetrate more kinds of glass than ordinary light.

▶ *This illustration shows the range of radiation in the electromagnetic spectrum. The waves are shown emerging from the Sun, as the Sun actually emits almost the full range of radiation. Fortunately, the atmosphere protects us from the dangerous ones.*

174

Gamma rays are dangerous high-energy rays with such short waves that they can penetrate solids. They are created in space and by nuclear bombs.

X-rays are longer waves than gamma rays but short enough to pass through most body tissues except bones, which show up white on medical x-ray photos.

The shortest ultraviolet rays in sunshine are dangerous, but longer ones give you a suntan in small doses. In large doses even long UV rays cause cancer.

Visible light varies in wavelength from violet (shortest) through all the colours of the rainbow to red (longest).

Infrared light is the radiation given out by hot objects. This is why infrared-sensitive 'thermal imaging' cameras can see hot objects such as people in pitch darkness.

Microwaves are used to beam telephone signals to satellites – and to cook food. Radars send out fairly short microwaves (about 1 cm long).

Television broadcasts use radio waves with waves about 0.5 m long.

Radio broadcasts use radio waves with waves from 300 m to 1500 m long.

Typical wavelength in metres or millimetres. Long waves are low frequency and low energy. Short waves are high frequency and high energy.

1 billionth mm

10 millionth mm

0.00001 mm

0.0005 mm

0.2 mm

0.3 m to 1 mm

0.5 m

300–1500 m

175

Einstein

- **Albert Einstein** (1879–1955) was the most famous and influential scientist of the 20th century.

- **Einstein was half German** and half Swiss, but when Hitler came to power in 1933, Einstein made his home in the USA.

- **Einstein's fame** rests on his two theories of relativity (see Relativity).

- **His theory of special relativity** was published in 1905 while he worked in the Patent Office in Bern, Switzerland.

- **In 1905** Einstein also explained the photoelectric effect. From these ideas, photo cells were developed. These are the basis of TV cameras and other devices.

▲ *Einstein's equation E=mc² revealed the energy in atoms that led to nuclear bombs and nuclear power.*

- **Einstein completed his theory** of general relativity in 1915 while Germany was at war.

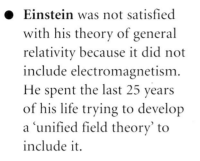

- **Einstein** was not satisfied with his theory of general relativity because it did not include electromagnetism. He spent the last 25 years of his life trying to develop a 'unified field theory' to include it.

- **Einstein** was once reported to have said that only 12 people in the world could understand his theory. He denied saying it.

- **Einstein** suggested to the US government that Germany was almost certainly developing an atomic weapon as World War 2 started. The US began developing one too.

- **Einstein was married twice.** His first wife was Mileva Maric. His second wife Elsa was also his first cousin.

▲ *A letter which Einstein wrote to President Roosevelt in 1939 led to the project to create the world's first atomic bomb.*

177

Time

- **No clock** keeps perfect time. For most of history clocks were set by the movement of the Sun and stars.

- **Since 1967** the world's time has been set by atomic clocks.

- **Atomic clocks** are accurate to 0.001 sec in 1000 years.

- **If a caesium atomic** clock ran for six million years it would not gain or lose a second.

- **The world's most** accurate clock is the American NIST-7 atomic clock.

- **The atomic clock** on the International Space Station is hundreds of times more accurate than clocks on Earth, because it is not affected by gravity.

- **Atomic clocks** work because caesium atoms vibrate exactly 9,192,631,770 times a second.

- **Some scientists** say that time is the fourth dimension – the other three are length, breadth and height. So time could theoretically run in any direction. Others say time only moves in one direction. Just as we cannot unburn a candle, so we cannot turn back time (see time travel).

- **Light takes** millions of years to reach us from distant galaxies, so we see them not as they are but as they were millions of years ago. Light takes a little while to reach us even from nearby things.

- **Einstein's theory of general relativity** shows that time actually runs slower nearer strong gravitational fields such as stars. This does not mean that the clock is running slower but that time itself is running slower. Time also goes slower as speed increases.

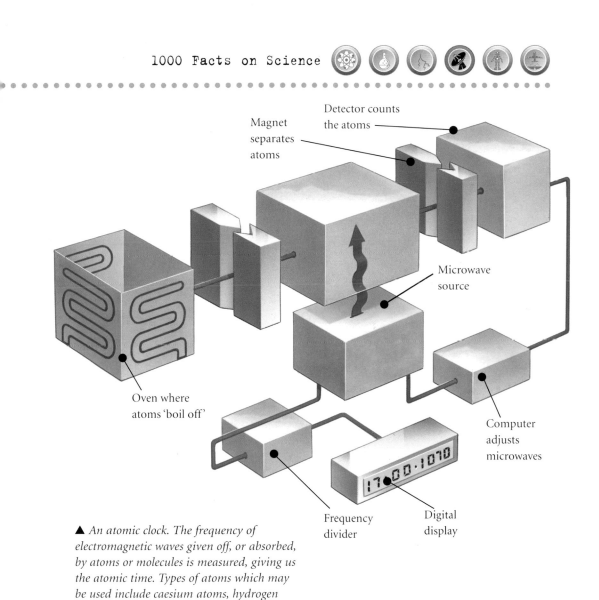

Detector counts
the atoms

Magnet
separates
atoms

Microwave
source

Oven where
atoms 'boil off'

Computer
adjusts
microwaves

17:00.1070

Frequency
divider

Digital
display

▲ *An atomic clock. The frequency of*
electromagnetic waves given off, or absorbed,
by atoms or molecules is measured, giving us
the atomic time. Types of atoms which may
be used include caesium atoms, hydrogen
atoms, and molecules of ammonia gas.

Time travel

- **Einstein showed** that time runs at different speeds in different places – and is just another dimension. Ever since, some scientists have wondered whether we could travel through time to the past or the future (see time).

- **Einstein said** you cannot move through time because you would have to travel faster than light. If you travelled as fast as light, time would stop and you would not be alive or even exist.

- **A famous argument** against time travel is about killing your grandparents. What if you travelled back in time before your parents were born and killed your grandparents? Then neither your parents nor you could have been born. So who killed your grandparents?

- **In the 1930s** American mathematician Kurt Gödel found time travel might be possible by bending space–time.

- **Scientists have come up** with all kinds of weird ideas for bending space-time, including amazing gravity machines. The most powerful benders of space-time are black holes in space.

- **Stephen Hawking** said you cannot use black holes for time travel because everything that goes into a black hole shrinks to a singularity (see Hawking). Others say you might dodge the singularity and emerge safely somewhere else in the Universe through a reverse black hole called a white hole.

- **US astronomer Carl Sagan** thought small black hole–white hole tunnels might exist without a singularity. There might be tunnels such as these linking different parts of the Universe, like a wormhole in an apple.

- **The mathematics** says that a wormhole would snap shut as soon as you stepped into it. However, it might be possible to hold it open with an anti-gravity machine based on a quantum effect called the Casimir effect.

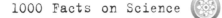 
- **Stephen Hawking** says wormholes are so unstable that they would break up before you could use them to time travel. Martin Visser says you might use them for faster than light (FTL) travel, but not for time travel.

The far end of a wormhole is the opposite of a black hole – a white hole. It pushes things out, not sucks them in.

The wormhole time machine depends on blowing a wormhole up large enough and holding it open long enough for you to slip through.

Although it's hard to imagine, space-time is not space with stars like this at all. It is a four-dimensional space and travelling through space-time means travelling through time as well as space.

If you could create a wormhole time machine, just where and when would the other end be?

▲ *If wormholes exist, they are thought to be very, very tiny – smaller than an atom. So how could they be used for time travel? Some scientists think you may be able to use an incredibly powerful electric field to enlarge them and hold them open long enough to make a tunnel through space-time.*

181

Space

- **A flat or plane surface** has just two dimensions at right angles to each other: length and width.

- **Any point** on a flat surface can be pinpointed exactly with just two figures: one showing how far along it is and the other how far across.

- **There are three** dimensions of space at right angles to each other: length, width and height.

- **A box** can be described completely with just one figure for each dimension.

- **A point in space** can be pinpointed with three figures: one shows how far along it is, one how far across it is and a third how high up or down it is.

▼ *An eclipse of the Sun in 1919 showed Einstein's suggestion that gravity can bend light is true. In bending light, gravity is also bending space–time.*

- **If something is moving,** three dimensions are not enough to locate it. You need a fourth dimension – time – to describe where the object is at a particular time.

- **In the early 1900s,** mathematician Hermann Minkowski realized that for Einstein's relativity theory you had to think of the Universe in terms of four dimensions, including time.

- **Four-dimensional** space is now called space-time.

- **Einstein's** theory of general relativity shows that space-time is actually curved.

- **After Minkowski's ideas,** mathematicians began to develop special geometry to describe four or even more dimensions.

▶ German mathematician Hermann Minkowski used geometrical methods to solve difficult problems in number theory, in mathematical physics and the theory of relativity.

183

Hawking

◀ *Stephen Hawking is one of the most famous living scientists. His computer-simulated voice is familiar on many TV science programmes.*

● **Stephen Hawking** (b.1942) is a British physicist who is famous for his ideas on space and time.

● **Hawking was born** in Oxford, England and studied at Cambridge University, where he is now a professor.

● **Hawking suffers** from the paralysing nerve disease called amyotrophic lateral sclerosis. He cannot move any more than a few hand and face muscles, but he gets around very well in an electric wheelchair.

● **Hawking cannot speak,** but he communicates effectively with a computer-simulated voice.

● **Hawking's** book *A Brief History of Time* (1988) outlines his ideas on space, time and the history of the Universe since the Big Bang. It was one of the best-selling science books of the 20th century.

▶ *Einstein thought of, and Hawking developed, the idea of black holes. They are collapsed objects, such as stars, that have become invisible.*

- **Hawking's contributions** to the study of gravity are considered to be the most important since Einstein's.

- **More than anyone else,** Hawking has developed the idea of black holes – points in space where gravity becomes so extreme that it even sucks in light.

- **Hawking developed** the idea of a singularity, which is an incredibly small point in a black hole where all physical laws break down.

- **Hawking's work** provides a strong theoretical base for the idea that the Universe began with a Big Bang, starting with a singularity and exploding outwards.

- **Hawking** is trying to find a quantum theory of gravity (see quantum physics) to link in with the three other basic forces (electromagnetism and nuclear forces).

◀ *The Big Bang theory assumes the Universe started with a singularity, a point of infinite mass and energy, but almost no size.*

Relativity

- **Einstein** (see Einstein) was the creator of two theories of relativity which have revolutionized scientists' way of thinking about the Universe: the special theory of relativity (1905) and the general theory (1915).

- **Time is relative** because it depends where you measure it from (see time). Distances and speed are relative too. If you are in a car and another car whizzes past you, for instance, the slower you are travelling, the faster the other car seems to be moving.

- **Einstein showed** in his special theory of relativity that you cannot even measure your speed relative to a beam of light, which is the fastest thing in the Universe. This is because light always passes you at the same speed, no matter where you are or how fast you are going.

- **Einstein** realized that if light always travels at the same speed, there are some strange effects when you are moving very fast (see below).

- **If a rocket** passing you zoomed up to near the speed of light, you would see it shrink.

▶ *In normal everyday life, the effects of relativity are so tiny that you can ignore them. However, in a spacecraft travelling very fast they may become quite significant.*

◀ *A spacecraft travelling almost at the speed of light seems to shrink. Of course, if you were actually on board everything would seem entirely normal. Instead, it would be the world outside that seemed to shrink, since it is travelling almost at the speed of light relative to you.*

- **If a rocket** passing you zoomed up to near the speed of light, you'd see the clocks on the rocket running more slowly as time stretched out. If the rocket reached the speed of light, the clocks would stop altogether.

- **If a rocket** passing you zoomed near the speed of light, it would seem to get heavier and heavier. But it gradually becomes so heavy, there isn't enough energy in the Universe to speed it up any further.

- **Einstein's general relativity theory** brought in gravity. It showed that gravity works basically by bending space-time. From this theory scientists predicted black holes (see Hawking) and wormholes (see time travel).

- **In 1919** an eclipse of the Sun allowed Arthur Eddington to observe how the Sun bends light rays, proving Einstein's theory of general relativity.

▼ *In a spacecraft travelling almost at the speed of light, time runs slower. So astronauts going on a long, very fast journey into space come back a little younger than if they had stayed on the Earth.*

◄ *In a spacecraft travelling almost at the speed of light, everything becomes heavier. Many scientists believe objects will never be able to accelerate to the speed of light because the faster it goes, the heavier it gets.*

...FASCINATING FACT...
When astronauts went to the Moon, their clock lost a few seconds. The clock was not faulty, but time actually ran slower in the speeding spacecraft.

187

Microscopes

- **Microscopes** are devices for looking at things that are normally too small for the human eye to see.

- **Optical microscopes** use lenses to magnify images by up to 2000 times.

- **In an optical microscope** an objective lens bends light rays apart to enlarge what you see; an eyepiece lens makes the big image visible.

- **Electron microscopes** magnify by firing streams of electrons at the object. The electrons bounce off the object onto a fluorescent screen which makes them visible.

- **An electron microscope** can focus on something as small as one nanometre (one-billionth of a millimetre) and magnify it five million times.

- **Scanning Electron Microscopes** (SEMs) scan the surface of an object to magnify it by up to 100,000 times.

▶ *In the 1660s, Robert Hooke much improved the compound microscope, a powerful scientific instrument which worked by using several lenses.*

▶ *A Scanning Electron Microscope clearly reveals the tiny nerve fibres inside the human brain.*

- **Transmission Electron Microscopes** shine electrons through thin slices of an object to magnify it millions of times.

- **Scanning Tunnelling Microscopes** are so powerful that they can reveal individual atoms.

- **The idea of electron microscopes** came from French physicist Louis de Broglie in 1924.

- **Scanning Acoustic Microscopes** use sound waves to see inside tiny opaque objects.

▶ *From the 1670s, Antoni Van Leeuwenhoek used his single lens microscope to study many different subjects: fibres of fabrics, leaves, small creatures, and human blood, skin and hair.*

189

Telecommunications

- **Telecommunications** is the almost instantaneous transmission of sounds, words, pictures, data and information by electronic means.

- **Every communication system** needs three things: a transmitter, a communications link and a receiver.

- **Transmitters** can be telephones or computers with modems (see the Internet). They change the words, pictures, data or sounds into an electrical signal and send it. Similar receivers pick up the signal and change it back into the right form.

- **Communications links** carry the signal from the transmitter to the receiver in two main ways. Some give a direct link through telephone lines and other cables. Some are carried on radio waves through the air, via satellite or microwave links.

- **Telephone lines** used to be mainly electric cables which carried the signal as pulses of electricity. More and more are now fibre optics (see fibre optics) which carry the signal as coded pulses of light.

- **Communications satellites** are satellites orbiting the Earth in space. Telephone calls are beamed up on radio waves to the satellite, which beams them back down to the right part of the world.

- **Microwave links** use very short radio waves to transmit telephone and other signals from one dish to another in a straight line across Earth's surface.

- **Mobile phones** or cellular phones transmit and receive phone calls directly via radio waves. The calls are picked up and sent on from a local aerial.

- **The information superhighway** is the network of high-speed links that might be achieved by combining telephone systems, cable TV and computer networks. TV programmes, films, data, direct video links and the Internet could all enter the home in this way.

▼ *This illustration shows some of the many ways in which telecommunications are carried. At present, TV, radio and phone links are all carried separately, but increasingly they will all be carried the same way. They will be split up only when they arrive at their destination.*

...FASCINATING FACT...
Calls across the ocean go one way by satellite and the other by undersea cable to avoid delays.

TV and radio signals are broadcast as pulses of radio waves, sent direct via cables or bounced off satellites.

Computer data are translated by a modem into signals that can be carried on phone lines.

Signals from individual transmitters are sent on from a telephone exchange or a service provider.

More and more communications are beamed from antenna dishes on the ground to satellites in space.

Telephones can link in to the phone network by a direct cable link. Mobile phones link through the air to local relay towers by radio waves.

Television

- **Television relies** on the photoelectric effect – the emission of electrons by a substance when struck by photons of light. Light-sensitive photocells in cameras work like this.

- **TV cameras** have three sets of tubes with photocells (reacting to red, green and blue light) to convert the picture into electrical signals.

- **The sound signal** from microphones is added, and a 'sync pulse' is put in to keep both kinds of signal in time.

- **The combined signal** is turned into radio waves (see electromagnetic spectrum) and broadcast.

- **An aerial** picks up the signal and feeds it to your television set.

- **Most TV sets** are based on glass tubes shaped like giant lightbulbs, called cathode-ray tubes. The narrow end contains a cathode, which is a negative electrical terminal. The wide end is the TV screen.

- **The cathode** fires a non-stop stream of electrons (see electrons) at the inside of the TV screen.

◀ *TV cameras convert a scene into an electrical signal.*

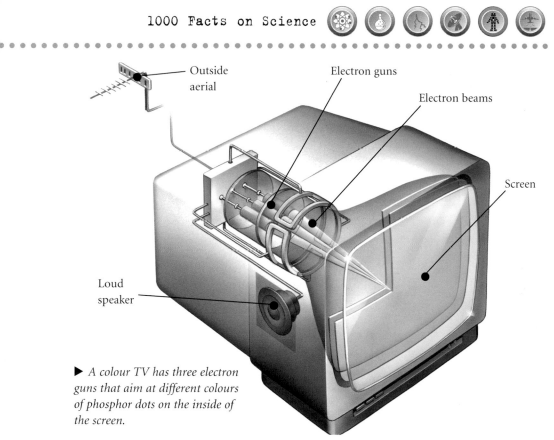

Outside aerial

Electron guns

Electron beams

Screen

Loud speaker

▶ *A colour TV has three electron guns that aim at different colours of phosphor dots on the inside of the screen.*

- **Wherever electrons** hit the screen, the screen glows as its coating of phosphors heats up.

- **To build up the picture** the electron beam scans quickly back and forth across the screen, making it glow in certain places. This happens so quickly that it looks as if the whole screen is glowing.

- **Colour TVs** have three electron guns: one to make red phosphors glow, another for green and a third for blue.

Scanners

● **Scanners** are electronic devices that move backwards and forwards in lines in order to build up a picture.

● **Image scanners** are used to convert pictures and other material into a digital form for computers to read.

● **A photoelectric cell** in the scanner measures the amount of light reflected from each part of the picture and converts it into a digital code.

● **Various scanners** are used in medicine to build up pictures of the inside of the body. They include CT scanners, PET scanners and MRI scanners.

● **CT stands** for computerized tomography. An x-ray beam rotates around the patient and is picked up by detectors on the far side to build up a 3-D picture.

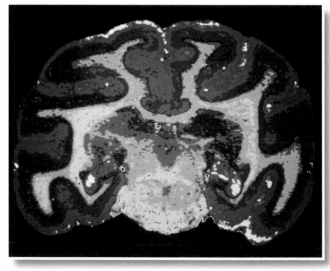

● **PET** stands for Positron Emission Tomography. The scanner picks up positrons (positively charged electrons) sent out by radioactive substances injected into the blood.

● **PET scans** can show a living brain in action.

▲ *This PET scan shows a monkey's brain from above.*

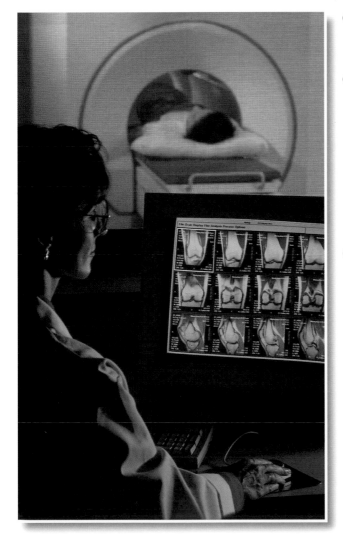

- **MRI** stands for Magnetic Resonance Imaging.

- **An MRI scan** works like CT scans but it uses magnetism, not x-rays. The patient is surrounded by such powerful magnets that all the body's protons (see atoms) line up.

- **The MRI scan begins** as a radio pulse that knocks the protons briefly out of alignment. The scanner detects radio signals sent out by the protons as they snap back into line.

◀ *A patient having an MRI scan. A computer converts signals from the scanner into images which it displays on a monitor.*

195

Computers

◀ *Created in the 1940s, the Colossus computer successfully cracked the German Enigma war codes.*

- **Part of a computer's** memory is microchips built in at the factory and known as ROM, or read-only memory. ROM carries the basic working instructions.

- **RAM** (random-access memory) consists of microchips that receive new data and instructions when needed.

- **Data can also** be stored as magnetic patterns on a removable disk, or on the laser-guided bumps on a CD (compact disc) or DVD (digital versatile disk).

- **At the heart** of every computer is a powerful microchip called the central processing unit, or CPU.

- **The CPU** works things out, within the guidelines set by the computer's ROM. It carries out programmes by sending data to the right place in the RAM.

◀ *Computers are developing so rapidly that models from the 1990s already look dated.*

- **Computers** store information in bits (binary digits), either as 0 or 1.

- **The bits 0 and 1** are equivalent to the OFF and ON of electric current flow. Eight bits make a byte.

- **A kilobyte** is 1000 bytes; a megabyte (MB) is 1,000,000 bytes; a gigabyte (GB) is 1,000,000,000 bytes; a terabyte (TB) is 1,000,000,000,000 bytes.

- **A CD can hold** about 600 MB of data – about 375,000 pages of ordinary text.

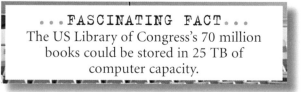

...FASCINATING FACT...
The US Library of Congress's 70 million books could be stored in 25 TB of computer capacity.

The Internet

- **The Internet** is a vast network linking millions of computers around the world.

- **The Internet began** in the 1960s when the US Army developed a network called ARPAnet to link computers.

- **To access the Internet** a computer's output is translated into a form that can be sent by phone lines with a modem (short for modulator/demodulator).

- **Computers** access the Internet via a local phone to a large computer called the Internet Service Provider (ISP).

- **Each ISP** is connected to a giant computer called a main hub. There are about 100 linked main hubs worldwide.

- **Some links between** hubs are made via phone lines; some are made via satellite.

- **Links between** hubs are called fast-track connections.

▼ *The Internet links computers instantly around the world.*

- **The World Wide Web** is a way of finding your way to the data in sites on all the computers linked to the Internet. The Web makes hyperlinks (fast links) to sites with the word you select.

- **The World Wide Web** was invented in 1989 by Tim Berners-Lee of the CERN laboratories in Switzerland.

▲ *E-mail, sending electronic messages from one computer to another, is used for business and pleasure.*

...**FASCINATING FACT**...
People can now access the Internet via mobile phones.

Sound recording

▶ *Microphones pick up sound waves and turn them into electrical signals. These are passed on to recording, amplifying or broadcasting equipment.*

- **Sound is recorded** by using a microphone to turn the vibrations of sound into a varying electrical current.

- **Sound recording** in the past was analogue, which means that the electrical current varies continually exactly as the sound vibrations do.

- **Most sound recording** today is digital, which means that sound vibrations are broken into tiny electrical chunks.

- **To make a digital recording** a device called an analogue-to-digital converter divides the vibrations into 44,100 segments for each second of sound.

- **Each digital segment** is turned into a digital code of ON or OFF electrical pulses.

- **With analogue sound,** each time the signal is passed on to the next stage, distortion and noise are added. With digital sound no noise is added, but the original recording is not a perfect replica of the sound.

- **On a CD (compact disc)** the pattern of electrical pulses is burned by a laser as a corresponding pattern of pits on the surface of the disc.

- **During playback,** a laser beam is reflected from the tiny pits on a CD to re-create the electrical signal.

- **DVDs** work like CDs. They can store huge amounts of data on both sides, but most can only be recorded on once.

- **Minidiscs** (MDs) use magneto-optical recording to allow you to record on the disc up to one million times. A laser burns the data into a magnetic pattern on the disc.

▲ *In a recording studio, the sound is recorded either on computer or on big master tapes.*

201

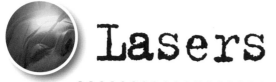

Lasers

- **Laser light** is a bright artificial light. It creates an intense beam that can punch a hole in steel. A laser beam is so straight and narrow that it can hit a mirror on the Moon.

- **'Laser'** stands for light amplification by stimulated emission of radiation.

- **Laser light** is even brighter for its size than the Sun.

- **Laser light** is the only known 'coherent' source of light. This means the light waves are not only all the same wavelength (colour), but they are also perfectly in step.

- **Inside a laser** is a tube filled with gases, such as helium and neon, or a liquid or solid crystal such as ruby.

- **Lasers work** by bouncing photons (bursts of light) up and down the tube until they are all travelling together.

- **Lasing begins** when a spark excites atoms in the lasing material. The excited atoms emit photons. When the photons hit other atoms, they fire off photons too. Identical photons bounce backwards and forwards between mirrors at either end of the laser.

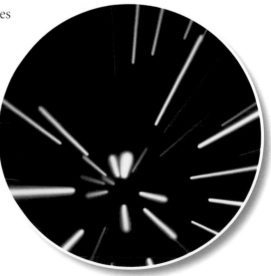

▶ *The amazingly tight intense beam of a laser is used in a huge number of devices, from CD players to satellite guidance systems.*

202

▶ *Lasers are used for delicate plastic surgery because the laser beam can be finely focussed and because its power can be carefully controlled.*

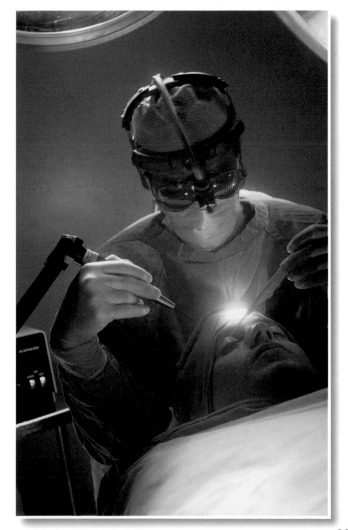

- **Gas lasers** such as argon lasers give a lower-powered beam. It is suitable for delicate work such as eye surgery.

- **Chemical lasers** use liquid hydrogen fluoride to make intense beams for weapons.

- **Some lasers** send out a continuous beam. Pulsed lasers send out a high-powered beam at regular intervals.

Fibre optics

- **Fibre optic cables** are bundles of transparent glass threads that transmit messages by light.

- **The light is transmitted** in coded pulses.

- **A thin layer of glass,** called cladding, surrounds each fibre and stops light from escaping.

▲ *A bundle of optical fibres glows with transmitted light.*

- **The cladding** reflects all the light back into the fibre so that it bends round with the fibre. This is called total internal reflection.

- **Single-mode fibres** are very narrow and the light bounces very little from side to side. These fibres are suitable for long-distance transmissions.

- **Aiming light** into the narrow core of a single-mode fibre needs the precision of a laser beam.

- **Multi-mode fibres** are wider than single-mode fibres. They accept LED (light-emitting diodes) light, so they are cheaper but they are unsuitable for long distances.

- **The largest cables** can carry hundreds of thousands of phone calls or hundreds of television channels.

- **Underwater fibre optic** cables transmit signals under the Atlantic and Pacific Oceans.

- **Optical fibres** have many medical uses, such as in endoscopes. These are flexible tubes, with a lens on the end, that are inserted into the body to look inside it. Optical fibres are used to measure blood temperature and pressure.

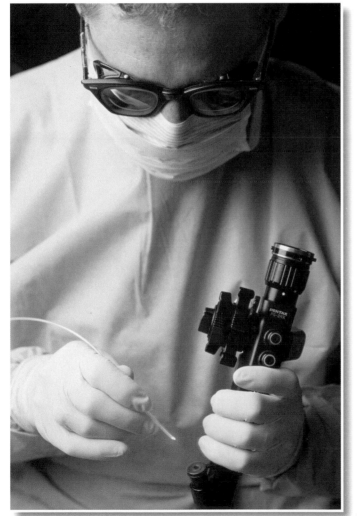

◄ *A laser endoscope is used for examining the inside of a patient. An optical fibre carries a laser beam which is used for precise surgery.*

205

Genetic engineering

- **Genetic engineering** means deliberately altering the genes of plants and animals to give them slightly different life instructions.

- **Genes** are found in every living cell on special molecules called DNA (deoxyribonucleic acid). Engineering genes means changing the DNA.

- **Scientists alter genes** by snipping them from the DNA of one organism and inserting them into the DNA of another. This is called gene splicing. The altered DNA is called recombinant DNA.

- **Genes are cut** from DNA using biological scissors called restriction enzymes. They are spliced into DNA using biological glue called DNA ligase.

- **Once a cell** has its new DNA, every time the cell reproduces the new cells will have the same altered DNA.

- **By splicing new genes** into the DNA of bacteria, scientists can turn them into factories for making valuable natural chemicals. One protein made like this is interferon, a natural body chemical which protects humans against certain viruses.

- **Scientists are now** finding ways of genetically modifying food crops. Crops may be engineered, for instance, to make them resistant to pests or frost. The first GM food was the 'Flavr Savr' tomato, which was introduced by the US biotechnology company Calgene in 1994.

> ...**FASCINATING FACT**...
> In 1999, scientists worked out the complete gene sequence for a multi-celled organism – allowing them to create a new organism artificially.

▲ *Genetic engineering may be used to make animals grow faster.*

- **Gene therapy** means altering the genes to cure diseases that are inherited from parents or caused by faulty genes.

- **Cloning** means creating an organism with exactly the same genes as another. Normally, new life grows from sex cells – cells from both parents – in which genes are mixed. Cloning takes DNA from any body cell and uses it to grow a new life. Since the new life has the same genes as the donor of the DNA, it is a perfect living replica.

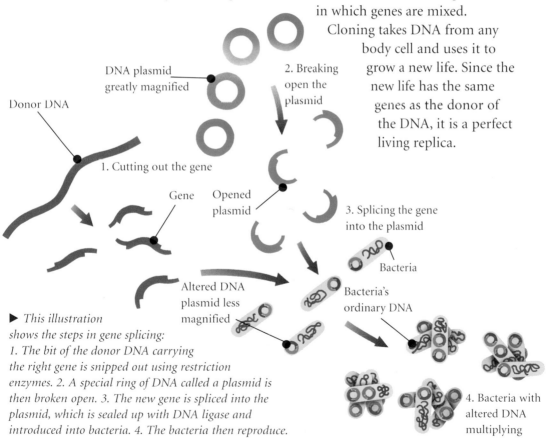

DNA plasmid greatly magnified

Donor DNA

2. Breaking open the plasmid

1. Cutting out the gene

Gene   Opened plasmid

3. Splicing the gene into the plasmid

Bacteria

Bacteria's ordinary DNA

Altered DNA plasmid less magnified

▶ *This illustration shows the steps in gene splicing: 1. The bit of the donor DNA carrying the right gene is snipped out using restriction enzymes. 2. A special ring of DNA called a plasmid is then broken open. 3. The new gene is spliced into the plasmid, which is sealed up with DNA ligase and introduced into bacteria. 4. The bacteria then reproduce.*

4. Bacteria with altered DNA multiplying

207

Index

Index

Index

Index

Index

Index

Index

Index

Acknowledgements

The publishers would like to thank the following artists who have contributed to this book:

Julie Banyard, Kuo Kang Chen, Nick Farmer, Mike Foster/Maltings, Alan Hancocks, Robert Holder, Rob Jakeway, Janos Marffy, Martin Sanders, Peter Sarson, Guy Smith, Sarah Smith, Rudi Vizi, Paul Williams, John Woodcock

The publisher would like to thank the following sources for the use of their photographs:

CASE Page 141; CORBIS: Page 205 Leif Skoogfors

All other pictures from the Miles Kelly Archives